The Population Activist's Handbook

The Population Activist's Handbook

The Population Institute

Macmillan Publishing Co., Inc.
New York

Collier Macmillan Publishers
London

Macmillan Publishing Co., Inc.
866 Third Avenue, New York, N.Y. 10022
Collier-Macmillan Canada Ltd.

Library of Congress Cataloging in Publication Data

Population Institute.
  Population: the activist's handbook.

  Bibliography: p.
  1. United States—Population—Handbooks, manuals,
etc. 2. Politics, Practical—Handbooks, manuals, etc.
I. Connolly, Gerald. II. Title.
HB3505.P63   301.32'9'73   73-21298
ISBN 0-02-598350-4
ISBN 0-02-053720-4 (pbk.)

First Printing 1974

Printed in the United States of America

Acknowledgments

The Population Activist's Handbook was written by
Gerald Connolly, Joan Draper, Leona Egeland, Beth Freeman,
Helaine Hamelstein, Kathryn Horsley, Roy Lucas,
Tracy Madden, Lynne Miller, Stephanie Mills, Deborah Oakley,
Daniel Pellegrom, Carl Pope, William Ryerson, Judy Senderowitz,
Kathleen Shordt, and Robert Wilson.
The general editor was Joan Draper.

The authors would like to thank the following people for their help in
making *The Population Activist's Handbook* a reality:
Yolande Baker, for typing and retyping the manuscript with infinite
care and patience; Peter Cott and Rodney Shaw, for their organizational
and inspirational support; and our editor, Amanda Vaill, for
putting it all together.

This book provides general guidance in the use of legal rights
and procedures for population-related problems. However,
in dealing with specific legal problems, the reader should obtain
the advice of a lawyer.

Contents

Foreword:

A Personal History by Stephanie Mills

Most people meditate in a lotus position—I meditate in the fetal position. Transcendental meditators get a two or three syllable mantra via episcopal succession from the Maharishi. My complex mantra—eco-catastrophe in all awful manifestations—comes via paperback and broadside from the guru Ehrlich. Some people chant *om* when they meditate. I just whimper—because four years ago I discovered the population explosion and have been worrying and wondering about it ever since.

Before then, I'd grazed peacefully in the field of literature, avoiding science; but there was no way to escape ecology, particularly in the San Francisco Bay area. A legislative battle over the establishment of a regional commission to protect San Francisco Bay had stimulated general environmental awareness; in addition to learning about environmental problems, we Californians began to notice the wealth of earthsaving organizations and institutions which had been in existence for years.

Sitting on the overstuffed couch in my dorm living room, I read *The San Francisco Chronicle* and became increasingly alarmed by reports of environmental deterioration. Ecology was not yet a hot student concern. Interested in learning more and sharing that information with the campus, I organized a panel which took place on what would be called Earth Day a year later. There were two token bad guys (or industry spokesmen, as they are also known), who were greatly outnumbered by good guys. It developed that there were two categories of good guys: establishment do-gooders (in this case represent-atives of local air and water pollution control districts) and radical do-gooders (Cliff Humphreys, who started Ecology Action; Marc Lappé, a speaker from Planned Parenthood; and Pete Zars, a devoted Sierra Club volunteer, as well as a fourth man, an experimental pathologist, whose name I have forgotten). The establishment do-gooders seemed to have greater rapport with the industry spokesmen than with the radicals. For one thing, they weren't nearly so worried; as far as they were concerned, there was plenty of time to clean up air and water without having to curtail industry too much, or abandon bureaucratic process.

The radicals brought nothing but bad news and a few times flatly contradicted the others. That there were such marked differences in styles of environmental problem-solving was news to me then—my first glimpse of a diversity (and divergence) that would become wider yearly. The symposium was new information even down to its hidden politics. However, it was poorly attended in spite of efforts to advertise it. A year later "ecology" anythings played to packed houses across the country.

It's interesting to speculate what the appeal of such an event would be today. My guess is that it would be small, a sermon to the converted, because the ecology/population craze is over, forgotten in the multitude of other problems besetting a failing economy. American social concerns manifest themselves as fads, and they stimulate general awareness only as long as the news media cover them.

The press, and television and radio, treat issues in much the same way that female praying mantises treat their male counterparts. They begin with a courtship dance, a concentrated paying of attention; then they have intercourse, in the midst of which the female bites the male's head off.

Clearly, there's no way to guarantee the effect of information. People have to be ready to learn and change, as I was in that last year of college. Late that night, after the panel, I happened to read, in one of the Sierra Club's recruiting packages, something that changed my life: Paul Ehrlich's potent broadside, "The Population Explosion—Fact or Fiction?" It focused my previously amorphous concern for the world's fate on the problem of overpopulation. It appeared to me then to be the most serious problem threatening mankind, and it still does.

At the time it wasn't much discussed publicly, so I wrote a graduation speech about the problem, and approached the friend whom I thought would be elected class speaker, offering my services as a ghost writer. She tossed my hat in the ring; I was elected, gave the address and became instantly famous for having made the drastic statement that this problem was so grave I would refuse to contribute to it by having children. After four years of being badgered by the question, "Are you really not?" my conviction is still firm; the answer's still no.

Having had ample occasion to consider childlessness, I like the idea. My guess is that as motherhood myths are more frequently challenged by the women's movement and by population pressure, more people will feel easier about opting for nonparenthood. This is a handbook of tactics for population activists. Employing the tactic of not having children means you're willing to put your body on the line for your belief. As I discovered, deciding not to behave in a conventional way is a fine opportunity to experience culture shock, but no one ever said that revolutionizing society would be *easy*, particularly for the revolutionaries.

The strain of consciously rejecting behavior which has hitherto been imperative for evolutionary survival is great, because humans are far more than merely conscious. The social strain is severe because revised behavior threatens people who don't choose to change, and threatened people can be *mean*.

Population control is a survival imperative which will rack societies that opt for practicing it, since it seems to be stronger and less acceptable to humans than the alternative— famine, plague or war-caused "die backs." Voluntary conscious social evolution is an altogether new challenge and humanity is slow to accept it.

Population growth statistics are quite as awesome today as they were four years ago. Few countries have achieved zero population growth, and the big nations which practice family limitation widely will be bigger still by the turn of the century. In twenty-five years, there will be millions more hungry, less arable land from which to feed them, fewer fish in the sea, dwindling supplies of nonrenewable resources. Perhaps the only commodity which increases will be hysteria. Presumably your interest in overpopulation has already dragged you through quantities of such bad news, so I'll conclude the recitation.

For about a year after my graduation I was a bad-news harbinger extraordinaire: Planned Parenthood of Alameda/San Francisco hired me as a campus organizer. My principal activity was speechmaking, and I visited campuses and organizations all over California and the West. This frequent lecturing was a challenge I was unprepared for, but I tried my best. One particularly trying try was an encounter with Tom Hayden, *Ur*-campus-lefty. We were both speaking at San Jose State University's orientation weekend. Frankly, I was awed by his presence, his fame and his radicalism. I had never quite been able to commit myself to the student radicalism then in fashion, and at that time saw it as my personal failing, really respecting the courage of those others who went out on limbs and proceeded to saw them off.

I spoke first, delivering a rousing exhortation to the incoming class to consider the gravity of the eco/population crisis and get to work alleviating it. The audience responded fairly well. I left the stage and we listened to two more speakers before the *pièce de résistance*.

Since this meeting was taking place shortly before the Chicago Seven trial, Tom Hayden dealt mainly with the circumstances which had led to the charge of conspiracy against him and his co-defendants, and with the ominous nature of the criminalization of the seven—all going on while America waged brutally senseless war against Indochina. Hayden's extemporizing was brilliant and original; his charisma derives as much from his intelligence as from his passion. I was suitably impressed until he mentioned, in passing, that the population problem was not nearly so serious as the war in Viet Nam and that the ecology movement was a bourgeois attempt to co-opt the Revolution.

I had to respond, but I hardly knew how. I was already defensive about the charge that population control was genocidal—it didn't (and doesn't) seem so to me, but so many worthy people were saying it was that I was confused. Then again, Hayden was a subculture hero, and although he was spouting half truths I was too intimidated to leap up and challenge them. When he had finished, I stood, quaking, to suggest that perhaps it was important to work on both these issues, that population pressure could make peace scarce even if the current war were over, that ecological problems affected rich and poor alike, that . . . that. . . .

Like any powerful politician, he was not willing to share a following and simply dismissed my arguments, continuing to rally the students to war protest. It was a case of "If you're not with us (down to the last iota of doctrine), you're agin us." A certain amount of factionalism can be a good thing, giving partisans a chance to get specific, making social ferment diverse, but the intolerance of the more-radical-than-thou and more-ecological-than-thou groups wastes energy. Tom Hayden, that day, was reluctant to take a longer view.

Now the war is said to be over, but the population explosion is not, though that class of San Jose State students, now graduating, may be oblivious to it, having had a gentle assist from the Left. If there is a Left, it's probably still toiling away on the Revolution, maybe hoping that the mounting pressure of hungry masses will magically tip the balance and precipitate global paradise. Apart from being terribly callous, the notion that people will not be moved to change until their situation becomes unbearable is ignorant of revolutionary history and the fact that there are already millions of people in unbearable situations whose limited energy must be devoted to mere survival. This argument against reform does not consider that the pressure of hungry masses all too often becomes a dead-weight of corpses.

It's ironic indeed, in the face of radical opposition to the population movement, that the People's Republic of China, conveniently detouring around Malthus, is using every means available to limit population growth. Contraception and abortion are free and universally available, thanks to the remarkable medical delivery system of barefoot doctors. Early marriage and families of more than two children are strictly discouraged. Even with these vigorous efforts to curb population growth, China can only hope to reduce her growth rate to one percent by the year 2000; one percent of eight hundred million is a multitude to feed on a finite Earth.

Given the colossal scale of these problems, what are we, personally, to do about them? This whole book tries to provide some answers. It provides strategies and tactics for infiltrating and changing existing systems (high school and college curricula, college health services), and for learning how you, the activist citizen, can use your representative government. As the book says, "We want you for the moment to accept the rules of the political game, the way it is actually played, not to debate what the rules ought to be."

That's all well and good if, by your vision of the present and future, you can accept *those* games. Bear in mind that big do-good organizations move slowly (if they are democratic) and pattern themselves after the (usually bigger) do-bad organizations. They are easily mired in organizational trivia and the seductive tedium of parlimentary procedures. If they do things too radically or manifest radical style, they imperil their all-important credibility. They must play by the other guy's rules. At best they create a safer climate for smaller, more drastic changes, and they reform the status quo.

If you are a do-gooder with your eye on the Big Picture, national or global institutions are likely your best option. One such is Planned Parenthood—World Population (PPWP), which has done good on the national scale in persuading the federal government to make family planning service available to medically indigent women in the United States, in addition to delivering a great deal of medical care through PP's clinics. Such million-dollar accomplishments are the aggregate of hundreds of minute, particular steps: years of dollars and census research, hundreds of face-to-face encounters with congressmen and their staffs, decades of struggle to establish and build respectability for a cause whose proponents were once jailed. One can't help but admire and be grateful for these solid accomplishments and services. On the other hand, one must also note that as PPWP expands its programs, it's developing a dependence on the U.S. Government's budget, and we are learning that the budget can be a whimsical thing where social, not military, programs are concerned. On the face of it, no other entity in the country has enough money to fund all the birth control services we need—what's the alternative?

Individuals can effect significant change; they are free to do radical things which, if they are intelligent, innovative and elegant, can have enormous impact. A case in point is Harvey Karman, a psychologist (not an M.D.), who has devoted much of his life to humanizing abortion. His recent revolutionary contribution is the Karman cannula, a flexible, blunt, small-bore plastic tube which is attached to a 50-cc syringe, inserted through the cervix (usually with no need for dilation). The plunger of the syringe is pulled and locked, thus creating a vacuum and effecting a vacuum-aspiration type abortion in minutes with virtually no danger of perforating the uterus.

Karman is a renegade inventor with absolute compassion. He didn't patent the device, which is inexpensive to manufacture, and he instructed his patients in its use so that they could perform abortions for other patients. This violates one of the unstated tenets of medical practice, that is, keeping knowledge and technique away from the consumer. The medical establishment has yet to officially approve this simple, useful tool, but women's groups and self-help clinics aren't waiting for such sanction—more and more of them are adopting menstrual extraction as a means of preventing unwanted births.

Another accomplishment of this non-doctor, undertaken simply to relieve human suffering but with significant implications for the field of population control, is his training of some four thousand paramedical workers in Bangladesh. Two hundred thousand women there had been raped during the 1971–1972 war: many were pregnant, all were considered defiled by this victimization, and thus they were outcast. Malcolm Potts, of the International Planned Parenthood Federation (IPPF), brought Karman there to instruct paramedics in the use of the supercoil technique. This technique involves the insertion of as many as eight IUDs in the uterus, where the IUDs expand and induce miscarriage. Side effects of this urgent act of mercy were the introduction to Bangladesh of a birth-control technology which cannot be ignored, and an expansion of women's options which cannot be revoked. The upshot has been a policy change. Bangladesh now has an abortion policy which is remarkably liberal. The moral of this story is that an individual with the courage to attempt problem-solving alone, outside the accepted system, *can* have a profound effect on national and global-scale problems.

The crises of overpopulation and environmental deterioration are really overwhelming, as is the variety of possible solutions. Selecting a mode of working on the problems which affords you a measure of integrity can be a mind-wrenching problem, particularly if you aren't the organization type. It's easy to get cowed by questioning the importance of small efforts: remarkable as they are, they seem small measured on the scale of the whole world. I would encourage you to know the importance of your own personal imagination and intelligence in solving any problem, lonely and small though you may seem in the face of legions of monstrous tasks.

Rather than try to convince you of that by exhortation, I offer the following eco-analogy:

There was once an era when earth was hospitable to dinosaur lifestyles. This planet must have thundered with the sound of their conflicts. Dinosaurs seem to have been in an arms race, growing ever larger and thicker-skinned, their monstrous scaly bodies sometimes vastly out of proportion to their brain size. Given favorable conditions, they could thunder around and rule the earth. But the earth changed somehow, and the dinosaurs passed on.

Before they went, however, some tiny newcomers had appeared on the scene—mammals. Surely a hot-blooded, furry little proto-possum would appear insignificant next to a Tyrannosaurus Rex. At first glance, the smart money would have been on the dinosaurs to win the evolutionary race. We know that things turned out differently. Something there was in that mammalian smallness which succeeded, and, after innumerable branchings of the evolutionary tree, became man. The proto-possums certainly quaked at dinosaur footfalls, but had the singular advantage of being easy to miss.

At this point in human history, the big institutions appear to be holding all the cards, including the capability of annihilating life on earth. The open question is whether to become commensurately big and powerful in order to avert disaster, or small and particular. Who could have foreseen the future of the possum?

Introduction: Why This Book?

A few years ago, concerned talk about the population crisis was a fashionable—and compelling—topic of conversation. We were running out of living space, our birthrates were soaring. Today there is rather less of that sort of talk: after all, birthrates in the United States seem to be declining, population density is low, people are leaving the central cities, and we still have enormous amounts of open space. It looks as if the population problem has gone away—or has it?

Whether birthrates are declining or not, the world's population will double by the year 2000. In all parts of the world more children are being born than can be adequately fed, clothed or housed; more people exist than can find jobs to support themselves. According to the *Report of the Commission on Population Growth and the American Future*, "this country, or any country, always has a 'population problem' in the sense of achieving a proper balance between size, growth, and distribution on the one hand, and the quality of life to which its citizens aspire on the other."

This book was written out of the conviction that it is high time someone did some sane thinking about the population problem. It assumes that you are that someone, and further assumes that you will want to do something about it. We have tried to provide you with the tools for the job: lists of publications, organizations, and individuals who can give you information or advice; models of successful citizen action undertaken by population-conscious groups across the country; suggestions for further action. Different sections of the book deal with changing population policy, promoting good population education, providing birth control and other population-related services for the community, encouraging population action in high schools, and achieving a sane international perspective on the population problem. Along the way we have touched on issues that may seem, at first glance, to have little to do with population *per se*. But, as the *Report* of the Commission says, "Population issues involve virtually every aspect of our national life. . . . Successfully addressing the population problem requires that we also address our problems of poverty, sex discrimination, minority discrimination, careless exploitation of resources, environmental deterioration, and decaying cities. The concern about population is as complex as it is consequential. There are no simple or immediate solutions. An attitude of indifference or complacency is unwarranted; so is the cry of early catastrophe and crisis."

To which we add: go to it.

Part One: Policy

Chapter One: The Population Policy Game

We have written this handbook as a guide to what we call the policy *game* not because population policy is not serious, not because we are not serious about it, nor yet because we do not hope that you will be serious about it. We have used the term and the language of games because we want you, for the moment, to accept the rules of the political game the way it is actually played, not to debate what the rules *ought* to be.

There is a game, an important one, whose proper object is the changing of the rules of political games in general, and it is the specialty of organizations like Common Cause, the American Civil Liberties Union, the Coalition for Congressional Reform and the League of Women Voters. But—and this is the irony of such organizations—even they must play by the rules they would like to change. And if you want to change population policy, you must do the same.

Our purpose then is to inspire you to effective action, not to arouse you with righteous indignation. We will try to retain confidence in your judgment to decide what ought to be, and limit ourselves to describing how it just might come to pass. Therefore, we may seem cynical, or crass. And we admit that when we play the policy games, we abandon the philosophy that says "It's not whether you win or lose." Too much is at stake; too much rides on the population policy game.

Population policy is the network of social customs, educational techniques, economic institutions and political rules by which society influences the decisions individuals make

about the size of their families and the size and structure of their communities. Policy includes all the actions of individuals or institutions which aim at influencing someone else's actions in some specified direction. In a sense, we all make policy. If I decide not to concern myself with population policy, to support what everyone else supports, I am choosing to support the demographic patterns which already exist.

The Elements of Policy

This handbook is written for those of you who reject the status quo population policy, and who want to try to change the habits of the American people in population matters. It will try to give you three things in addition to your broad goal:

☐ a specific target or targets: a list of elements in present population policy which you want to change;

☐ an idea of where you can find, and how you can utilize, the resources available to you to pursue that target; and

☐ a series of possible strategies, by which you may extend those resources to change that particular policy.

We often think of policy as a governmental function, but most population choices are made in families, businesses, churches, schools, and even individuals. Each of us controls, at the least, his own time and money and each of us, therefore, is a conscious supporter or reformer of the present population

1

status quo. The goal of this chapter is to make you a conscious policy maker, and an effective one.

Effectiveness is not strictly a matter of size. Americans have always felt that bigger is better and stronger is also better, so it has been easy to assume that bigger is stronger. Most of us run our daily lives on the principle that Goliath will win—a fairly common copout. People who say, "What's the use, they're too strong anyway," may be the biggest advantage the Goliaths of the world possess. This handbook is aimed at the unintim-

idated, the potential Davids. It is designed to help David win. As William Jennings Bryan put it, "Not all the hosts of error can prevail against the force of an idea whose time has come."

Strategies: the Use of Self-Interest

As we shall see, there are a lot of different population policies which, added together, determine the demographic shape of America. The one you pick to change will depend on who, and where, and when, you are; and in the rest of this chapter we will try to give you

NEW YORK TIMES/MICHAEL EVANS (AMERICAN FREEDOM FROM HUNGER FOUNDATION)

some insights into the different policy games that exist, the kind of resources you need to play them, and a few of the strategies that help to win them.

There is one general rule in playing the policy game: the critical measure of a good strategy is the extent to which it gives you influence over other people's reactions. It is rarely possible to force others to support you against their self-interest; that is a last resort. You can get farmers, lawyers, doctors and veterans to help you if you will figure out how population issues relate to their self-interest. Your first task is to determine whose help you need, and then to examine their self-interest; see if you can use it to convince them to do things your way, to spend their resources in a way which not only meets their needs, but helps change population policy in your direction.

One of the disadvantages of a big organization, like government, is that it is susceptible to exploitation by someone like you. Bigness means complicated structures; there is almost bound to be someone within the structure whose self-interest would be enhanced by the

changes you are working toward. Bigness also means routine, which means that big organizations often make a lot of their policy unconsciously. They are not very good at thinking out the connection between the way they spend their resources and the changes which actually result. This gives you the chance to outthink them and to encourage them to apply resources in a way which advances your goals instead of the organization's. The biggest organizations are difficult to beat, but they are the easiest to infiltrate and exploit.

> "Politics is the art of making the self-interest of cads closer to that of decent people."
> —Ambrose Bierce

Chapter Two: Elements of Population Policy

One surprising thing about population policy is that it embraces almost everything. The decision to have, or not to have, a child is one of the most complex choices a person can make, and it is a choice occasioned by a wide variety of influences. Look at some of the ways in which governmental and nongovernmental policies affect birth rates:

Can What You Don't Know Hurt You?

One of the crucial factors in deciding how many children you will have is the adequacy of the contraceptives which are available. There is no perfect contraceptive. The bulk of basic medical research in most areas is sponsored by the federal government through the National Institutes of Health (NIH). In recent years, most of the disease-fighting or life-saving advances in medicine have had their origins in work funded out of NIH.

By contrast, the federal government's involvement in improving contraceptives is recent in origin, minimal in scope, and lackadaisical in pace. All the recent advances in contraception, including oral contraceptives (the Pill) and the various intra-uterine devices, were developed by the private sector.

There is now a population research program within the National Institutes of Health, but it has never been funded at the level needed to make a difference. While programs of cancer research, for example, are often funded at levels which insure that all researchers whose requests are judged worthy will get money, the Center for Population Research in recent years has funded only about

50 percent of the grants which it approved. Because population research programs got a late start, they must *grow* more rapidly than other areas of medical research if they are to catch up. But such rapid growth generates suspicion and hostility from medical researchers in other- fields, who are often in positions to stifle the growth of population research programs. For example, it is often argued that it would be wasteful to increase spending on contraceptive research too rapidly, because there are not enough trained researchers to work on the problems. At the same time, the health bureaucracy denied the Center for Population Research adequate funds to train researchers. It's Catch-22.

Who pays? Well, anyone who suffers serious side effects from using the Pill or an IUD pays first. And lots of people pay because they used contraceptives which didn't work, and some women became pregnant. Perhaps some had abortions, which minimized the long-term cost; but perhaps some chose to, or had to, bear the child, who may suffer the significant psychological problems that go with being unwanted. The parents may pay with the disruption of their schooling, the loss of the mother's job, or the wiping out of their savings due to the unwanted and unplanned pregnancy.

Another facet of policy which influences or dictates the individual's decision about whether or not to have a child is the denial of birth-control information. State governments are among the worst offenders in this regard. For example, Michigan has a statute which prohibits the teaching of birth control (contraception) to students in the public schools, a statute which effectively prevents many young people from having any access to birth-control information. The high number of unplanned and often unwanted pregnancies among young women in school indicates a need for contraceptive education. The high increase in illegitimacy in Michigan causes considerable concern on the part of public health officials, both for the mother and the child. The illegitimacy *rate* has increased 197 percent in the last ten years. Many of these births occur among teenagers. Yet young persons who may be sexually active and who want to behave responsibly are not given information to protect themselves from pregnancy or venereal disease.

This policy has ramifications beyond a rising birth rate. In the past decade (1960–1969), gonorrhea has increased 98 percent in Michigan, with 8372 reported cases in 1960 and 18,523 reported cases in 1969. Clearly, gonorrhea is seriously increasing—and reported cases are the minimal number, since many cases of venereal disease are never reported at all.

A survey of college students in Michigan, in the spring of 1970, revealed that parents were seldom their source of information concerning either human reproduction or contraception. Regarding contraception instruction, 80 percent received *none* from their mothers. The role the school must play in the absence of education at home seems obvious. Yet Michigan is not the only state which still

has this kind of prohibition by statute.

Do People Buy Their Children From Madison Avenue?

In recent years, advertisers on television and in magazines and newspapers have been more restrained about touting the virtues of large families along with those of their product. But large families are still getting prizes for being large; having a baby turns you on to a great new product; other products bring order to the chaos of large family life by making daily chores so easy. You see the easy affluence of large families as they get together in model kitchens and drive off in $7,000 cars.

Why? Because in advertising, if you are reaching out to a large, diverse audience, you look for the least controversial subjects for your vehicle. And traditionally, one of the least controversial subjects on the American scene is the family—or rather the large, happy family. Business, it appears, is more than willing to use its advertising dollar to encourage large families—and when you buy the product, you foot the bill!

Up to the last three years, general interest magazines, women's magazines and television shows have focused largely on the joy and security of family-life-with-kids. Women on game shows are still asked how many children they have and the audience applauds furiously when the number is unusually large. Magazine fiction, situation comedies, and made-for-television movies often feature couples having problems which are resolved in the

end by pregnancy—despite statistical evidence that pregnancy usually heightens existing problems in a marriage.

In both magazines and television we see examples of large, trouble-free families—the Partridge Family and the Brady Bunch lead idyllic lives. And it is not uncommon for a long-established fictional family to "liven things up" with the addition of a new baby.

Times are changing, though. One indication of a reversal of some of television's pronatalist attitudes was Tandem Production's "Maude" show. Maude opted for abortion over late middle-aged motherhood. Soap operas, as well, are beginning to highlight alternative lifestyles instead of perpetual pregnancy. Newspapers are paying increasing attention to population matters, generally in enlightened contexts. But the edge of reform is ragged. Until the 1972–73 Planned Parenthood TV campaign, birth control was practically unheard of in the media. Even today, night clubs and topless bars get newspaper advertising space more readily than family planning clinics.

The Groves of Academe

Another influence on family size is the mass of social roles and expectations which assume that women have as their primary purpose in

BERNE GREENE

life the bearing and rearing of children. When social institutions arrange their rewards, rules and priorities on the assumption that half of the population is going to spend its time having children, the likely result is that a good many women will end up having children because they do not have easily attainable alternatives. Among the social institutions most blatantly pursuing this assumption are colleges and universities.

To begin with, most educational institutions do not provide adequate contraceptive services. Since students, in many cases, are from out of town and may not know where to get medical treatment outside the uni-

versity, the universe of medical care available to them is that of the student health service. And most health services still believe that the absence of good reproductive and sexual medical care will prevent sex and pregnancy.

Even when a couple has access, in or out of the university, to contraception, the institution still adopts policies geared to the assumption that they do not. Quotas and other devices which discriminate against the hiring of women, or the granting to them of financial aid, are justified in terms of the inconvenient possibility that the woman will not be a serious employee or student because she may become pregnant. Many schools main-

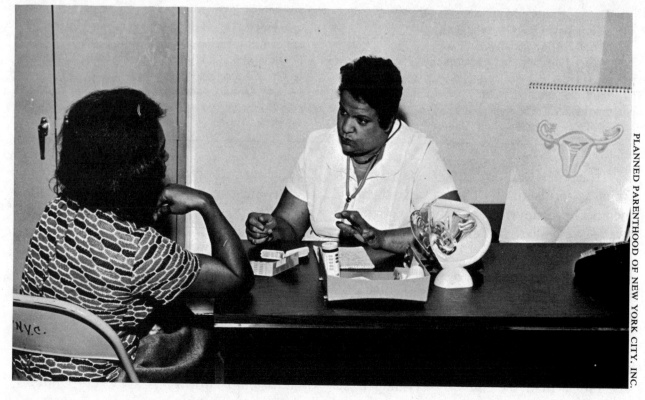

Population Policy Checklist

Prevailing population policy is often hard to gauge, but unless you know what your targets are you may find hitting them is impossible once the shooting starts. This checklist may help you to take aim more accurately.

1. What sort of population-related information is available to the public? Look for
☐ School or college programs in sex education
☐ Public display of contraceptives with information on their use
☐ Requirements that instructions be enclosed with birth-control devices such as condoms
☐ Distribution of birth-control information in doctors' offices and clinics
☐ Laws requiring that birth control information be handed out with marriage licenses

2. Does the public have access to birth-control devices and technology? Check on
☐ Abortion laws and practices
☐ Age of consent for prescription of contraceptives
☐ Hospital restrictions on who may have an abortion or a sterilization operation
☐ Policies of Catholic hospitals toward contraception and sterilization
☐ Laws which restrict sales of contraceptives to minors, or limit such sales to pharmacies

3. What kind of financing is there for population programs? Look for
☐ Government-run or government-funded clinics, referral services, pregnancy testing services or information services
☐ Availability of all methods of fertility control in both private and state-financed health insurance programs

4. How prevalent, and how powerful, are pro-natalist attitudes in your community? Consider
☐ Educational biases, support for the baby cult in school family-life courses, sexism in textbooks, treatment of population matters in school and college texts
☐ Public and private treatment of men's and women's roles, state ratification of the Equal Rights amendment, hiring policies
☐ Discrimination against the unmarried in tax, credit or housing policies
☐ Unwarranted subsidies—in taxation, housing, transportation, etc.—for families with many children

tain rules against "nepotism," one effect of which is to insure that the wife of a faculty member in a university town will find it almost impossible to find employment. Spouses of students are charged out-of-state tuition fees at many state universities. This effectively prices many women out of higher education.

Even though the universities act on the assumption that a woman is indeed likely to have one child, they rarely, if ever, rearrange their customs to make this a viable choice for her rather than the end of everything else.

Classes and library hours are often scheduled inconveniently for part-time students, creating a self-perpetuating myth that mothers and wives can't make it in academe. Fringe benefits for part-time employment are either non-existent or minimal. Charges for students who attend part-time are usually higher, on a course-by-course basis, than for full-time students.

The same things hold true—perhaps in even greater measure—in the business and professional worlds. Large corporations, which are by nature more rigidly structured in their schedules than most universities are, certainly are not hospitable to the working mother. And health plans in most corporations, large or small, tend to be pro-natalist and sexist. These health plans don't usually cover abortions or birth-control medication, although they do make allowances for hospitalization, doctor's bills, and medical costs for births. Futhermore, they often pay less— in terms of benefits and compensated time off the job—to female employees than to wives of male employees.

On the university campus or in the professional and business community, such accumulated failures to respond to human needs lead many women—whether they are students or not—to abandon the idea of working because too many of the cards are stacked against them.

This, then, is what you're up against when you decide you want to do something about the population problem. You must learn how to play the policy game as well as, or better than, other people do; learn to substitute your policy for theirs. But to play the game at all, you need a team—and in the next chapter we've tried to show you how to put it together.

Chapter Three: Putting Your Team Together and Keeping It Together

You *can* play the policy game alone; but even Don Quixote enlisted the aid of Sancho Panza, and you are much more likely to thrive as a policy maker if you organize a team to help you out. You should start with those who agree with you before you try to change those who disagree. Leaders without active followers do not constitute a movement. A few isolated people operating at full steam can achieve only isolated success unless they recruit followers. The leadership core needs some kind of structure, some assigning of responsibility to its members. But the key to morale is to make that structure as open and as free from elitism as possible. If you have a steering committee, it should rarely, if ever, meet in private. The politics of the closed door are the politics of turning people off.

Logistics

Bring as many activists into your effort as possible; have specific tasks to assign them; and make sure that their efforts are rewarded, both intrinsically (by success) and formally (through praise and recognition). Graduate good people from busy-work as quickly as possible, though you probably will have to start them there. Make sure that every member of your steering committee does a good deal of his or her own dirty work. Your ability to pass on responsibility is critical; you give more people a stake in success and you take the pressure off your starting group. Remember that there is no need for anyone to lack a title for use in phone conversations. Use a thesaurus if necessary. No one should have to answer the phone and say, "Well, I'm just a volunteer."

Think of your organization in dynamic terms. The important question is "what are our members doing?" not "what is the structure of our organization?". The key lines in your head need to be "who talks to, walks with, eats with, telephones who," not "who is in charge of the committee." Ideas and information are the keys to motivation; don't hog them.

Every task contributes to your organization in two ways; it makes a direct contribution when it is completed, but while it is going on, it is developing the skill of your people. The second function is easy to overlook, but important. Try giving assignments to people who will learn the most by doing them, not always to those who may do the most polished job.

Where do you seek your followers, and who should they be? Only a small percentage of potential followers are potential activists. Your first priority is to find people who will make substantial commitments of time and energy to changing population policies. But you will eventually need the help of a larger, less dedicated following—a group which can be called on in emergencies, which increases the potential for financial or political support, and which will yield a surprising number of second-generation leaders.

Interest in playing on your policy game team is likely to come from two groups: people who have particular knowledge about the policy you want to change and people who have been particularly affected by it. If you're trying to get a gynecologist assigned to the staff of your school or college health service, try to locate women who have had to resort to outside medical assistance in a crisis. And search for sympathetic support at the medical schools in the area or among the gynecologists who carry the burden in the absence of a health service doctor. A battle over local population growth might appeal to planners, as well as to residents who are bothered by a particular traffic jam or proposed development. The more directly an individual is in-

volved in a policy issue, the more likely he or she is to lead.

In recruiting followers, remember that people like to join the winning side, or at least "*a good outfit.*" Your own seriousness about what you are trying to do, your self-confidence that it is important and worthwhile, are your biggest assets. Don't be afraid to ask people for support and/or money. Put the burden on them to refuse you; "Why haven't you joined?" is much more effective than "Is there any chance you could help us?"

Displays of spirit and concern attract people at the beginning, but these cannot remain

COMMON CAUSE

the sum of your activity. While a speaker or a film may sustain momentum, a continuous diet of such events will turn people away faster than anything except a continuous diet of meetings. Most people want to do something; it's imperative that programs and activities expand as fast as your support base.

Keep your structure fluid and flexible. Don't waste time with intricate by-laws and charters. Never let your structure keep you from doing something you consider worthwhile. Your steering committee should be open to people pushing new ideas; your officers should be *workers*. Use an advisory or honorary board if you have big names to exploit—and splash them on your stationery. (Invest in a letterhead if you do much writing to people you care about; 1000 sheets will cost less than ten dollars if you can get a friendly artist or designer to put in the labor.)

Committees are great, if they work. Don't waste time trying to make them work. Organize your committees around tasks, not around subject areas. You only need a standing committee where you have a standing relationship with the outside; if you lobby regularly, for instance, you need a committee of lobbyists. Otherwise, form a committee for a particular job and disband it when that job is finished. It does help to have *individuals*

charged with overseeing broad areas of responsibility. The key time in a committee's life is the two weeks after its members sign up. If you don't get them involved then, you may never be able to do so; if they start giving five hours a week then, you may never be able to discourage them.

A telephone, with a listed number, is almost always worth the money; you might also invest in an answering service (cheaper than you may think), if you don't have any other way to have the phone covered. (Can you share a line with another organization which can answer when you're not there?)

An office is a big boost if it fits into the budget. It gives the group credibility and substance, and offers new recruits a focal point. See if you can get free space from a university, a church or a sympathetic merchant. Try to get friendly offices to donate supplies. Hold a housewarming party with a blatant appeal for gifts. ZPG/NY (the New York Chapter of Zero Population Growth) did this with a detailed suggestion list ranging from paper clips to Xerox machines. No one offered a Xerox, but it took them three years to run out of paper clips.

To Get Money

No worthwhile game can be played in bank-

COMMON CAUSE

ruptcy. One of the oldest con games for getting money is forming a bogus corporation and selling shares. You can use the same ploy by setting up a real organization and charging dues. But good activists are generally better used working hard than being hit for high dues; you probably can't run your efforts on the bootstraps of the same people that man them. Sales of promotional materials such as buttons, books, bumper stickers, T-shirts and posters yield publicity as well as cash. You can set a good profit margin if you have designers, seed money for production, and volunteers who will hawk your message. In an emergency, pass the hat at a meeting. Get someone to kick the donations off blatantly by showing a five- or ten-dollar bill. Then embarrass everyone else into giving. But it's always better to get money from outsiders than to wear down devoted followers.

Mailings are good, for both recruitment and money. You get a better return if you raise money for a particular purpose, like a special ad campaign or a legislative fight. Potential donors have a better idea of what product you are selling them. Use a test mailing to check out potential target groups. Raffles can work well, especially if the prizes are donated. Try to get prizes that the general public will want, so that you can tap the largest possible audience. Vacation trips are particularly enticing.

In certain areas, garage sales of donated items work very well. You need a garage of sorts, free saleables, *good* publicity and responsible organizers. Every group, from rad-

ical plumbers to Camp Fire Girls, tries bake sales, and the returns are usually low. It's foolish to spend forty hours in preparation and work to make forty dollars—better to go out and work those hours for minimum wage and donate the income. (Incidentally, if you have more people than you need who want to work for you at low salaries, see if you can get some of them to take better-paying jobs and donate four hours' worth of their weekly wages.)

Remember, it's much easier to get money if you can point to what you have accomplished and what you will do with more funds. Your programs should be ready to begin as soon as you raise the money. Don't be afraid to go to industry, community organizations and even government agencies for money or contributions in kind. Don't be afraid to ask for help when you have a good cause.

Communicating Within the Team

Once you have your members, and a certain amount of cash to back them up, you must decide how they should communicate. Meetings are necessary—at least, everyone thinks so. Most organizations set up a meeting schedule and let it run the organization into the ground. The steering committee may need to meet every week at the start, but even this becomes a waste of time at some point. Conference telephone calls are easier, and have less tendency to become incestuous show-and-tell exercises.

If meetings continue to increase the commitment and energy of those who attend, or if they attract new recruits who become converts, they are productive. Otherwise, call your people together only when you need to solve problems.

Regular meetings often tend to become a substitute for an office or a telephone to give the organization "substance." Members need to be reassured that they are part of a group endeavor. If this is unavoidable, offer something interesting: a good speaker, a film or, perhaps best, a pot-luck supper. A meeting format that forces your activists to be passive will leave them passive after the meeting; your goal is to charge them up.

There are more efficient devices for communication than meetings. If there is a fairly large, stable following, a cheap newsletter is a good investment. If you mail more than 200, you can save on postage by using a bulk rate; put some of your savings into offset printing. Use your logo on the masthead. This is much more likely to be read than a mimeographed sheet. Use your newsletter as an action device; tell your members specifically what to do. Don't just announce whom they can call to find out what to do, or the meeting they can attend. Give your orders right there!

Your newsletter needs an editor, and the editor needs total responsibility, but other steering committee members must keep the editor informed. The editor should put action targets and other regular features in the same spot each issue and should avoid padding. If you don't have enough hard news, you are publishing too often. (Or you're doing too little.)

Suppose that, at the end of the legislative session, your state legislature introduces a bill to establish a state population commission. The vote is scheduled for tomorrow, and you have twenty-four hours to send an avalanche of pro-commission telegrams and telephone calls to your legislators. Impossible? Not if you use a telephone tree, a device by which A calls B, C, D, and E, and B, in turn, calls F, G, H, and I. The telephone tree can save your life in an emergency like this.

Divide your activists into groups of eight to ten, with branch leaders. (Use logical divisions like dormitories or assembly districts, if possible.) Each branch leader should have a complete list of his or her contacts, with all possible phone numbers and addresses and a stack of postcards to use when he/she can't get through by phone. The leader should report all changes in the list to the steering committee. This is also a good way to involve members who don't come to meetings for reasons of time, geography or personal preference. Use the tree at regular intervals, to keep it running smoothly. When you activate, make sure your branch leaders really understand your tactics. They will slack off if they feel insecure in their mission.

Team Morale

Grass-roots activists lose battles when they get disheartened. Defeat can destroy morale, but loneliness is ten times deadlier. Especially during the planning period, symbols help to make recruits feel part of something. Use a slogan or a graphic design on all your buttons, posters and literature, and be sure to wear these symbols at any public appearances.

True victories don't come often. The policy game is time-consuming, and it's important to set symbolic benchmarks for yourself and the troops. Measure your progress against these, and don't be afraid to declare a victory, even a small one. Medals, or whatever forms of reward you use, help reinforce your troops.

Don't be afraid of giving out too many, as long as you give them to the real workers, regardless of rank.

An army travels on its stomach, but it fights on friendships. Parties, assuming they help build friendships, are good tactics. You can use them to advance an organizational goal as well—recruitment, raising money, starting a raffle, or introducing a candidate for office. Puritanism is one of the occupa-

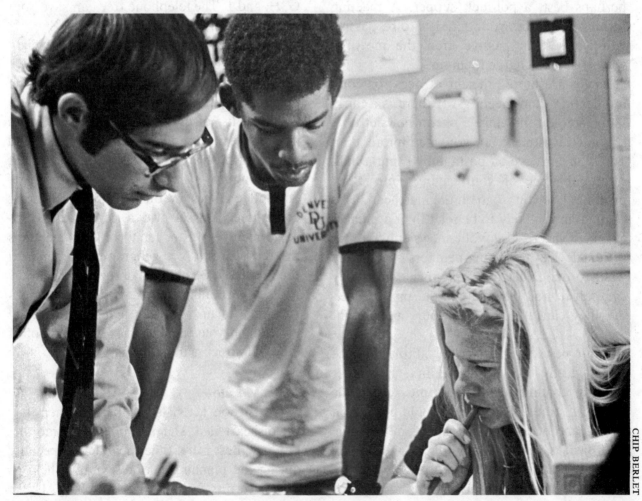

CHIP BERLET

tional diseases for would-be policy makers, so that having a "reason" for a party may satisfy that hang-up as well.

In all of this, remember that your basic resource is the people who believe in what you're doing, who want to affect population policy. Their value is only in small part a function of their numbers and the first way to increase their value is to increase their commitment. That calls for a group with a strong sense of purpose, good working relations, careful delegation of responsibility, and lots of mutual admiration. Avoid formations and operations that say to people, "we happy few," "I know better," "we don't need you right now, come back next week," and "if you want to help, find your own job."

Once your people are committed, they need skills. You can help provide them. A speakers' bureau, for example, can be either great or a drag, depending on the quality of the information and guidance available to its members. The speakers' manual should be regularly updated with new information and sample speeches for new members; you should hold workshops where the opposition's arguments are brought up and answered by different speakers; and you should seek reactions from groups you speak to on the quality of your speech.

If your group is going to start lobbying, get some training from someone who has lobbied before—perhaps from an environmental group or the League of Women Voters. Try role-playing; test your core of lobbyists out on mock "hostile" legislators. See that they can keep their cool and answer the other side effectively—which, after all, is what effective population action is all about.

Chapter Four: Some Notes on the Other Players

Once you've got yourself organized, it's time to take on the outsiders, but before you go into action it's best to familiarize yourself with the other players in the population policy game.

Notes on Your Targets

The U.S. Congress can be one of the most frustrating targets for anyone working to influence population policy. For a long time, Congress was terrified of population issues, because it was terrified of sex, and it is only in the past five years that even a minority of Congressmen have been willing to talk publicly about issues like contraception and abortion.

Yet Congress is absolutely critical in population policy. Among the specific areas under the jurisdiction of Congress are federal research into contraceptive technology, and other aspects of the population problem; federal funding of birth-control programs for low-income families; the inclusion of birth-control services in national health care programs; immigration; foreign aid in the population field; and population education. Most important, Congress is in a position to insure that federal programs in all areas will be designed with the population problem in mind, just as the 1970 National Environmental Policy Act requires all federal activities to be planned with environmental quality in mind. So, whatever your area of concern, if federal money enters into it in some way, Congress has something to say about it.

There are a number of things to remember in getting Congress to say what you want. First, most Congressmen, including many Senators, are specialists, putting most of their time and energy into work on their committees. To change a policy in the field of education, you need the help of a Senator or a Representative on the education committee. The attitudes of other members only matter if your bill comes to the floor for a final vote.

Second, there is virtually no way that a citizen's group in Kansas can directly influence a Senator from Massachusetts; letters from the 1st District of Michigan will mean little to the Representative from the 5th District. To influence a given Congressman, you need to influence his constituents, and get *them* to build the pressure.

Third, always appeal to your Congressman on the basis of the validity of your case; the signature at the bottom of your letter is what must convince him that his constituents will support him if he does as you ask. Never threaten: it only shows you are weak.

Fourth, letters are effective but personal contact is more effective. Visit your Congressman at his office in Washington, or when he comes back to the district. Show up at rallies and speeches and ask your questions—show your posters. Find out which of your friends know him personally, which have his trust and confidence. Find out what particular constituent groups get along best with him: farmers, lawyers, doctors, veterans. Get them to help you.

Fifth, in deciding whether to go to a Senator or a Representative, remember that most

---

Zeroing in on the Congress

Some member of the Congress have openly expressed sympathy toward the goals of population groups, either by voting for bills that make good population sense or, in some cases, by working to generate good population legislation. On population issues generally, Senator Robert Packwood of Oregon and Congressman Paul McCloskey of California have good track records. On family planning issues, the following have been sympathetic:

Alan Cranston (Senator from California)
Jacob Javits (Senator from New York)
Bella Abzug (Representative from New York)
George Brown (Representative from California)
Ron Dellums (Representative from California)
Pierre Dupont (Representative from Delaware)
Robert Eckhardt (Representative from Texas)
Pat Schroeder (Representative from Colorado)
Frank Horton (Representative from New York)

Lobbies that have worked for population legislation in the Congress are:

ZPG Washington Office
1346 Connecticut Avenue N.W.
Washington, D.C. 20036

National Organization for Women (NOW)
1107 National Press Building
Washington, D.C. 20004

Women's Lobby
1345 G Street S.E.
Washington, D.C. 20003

Common Cause
2030 M Street N.W.
Washington, D.C.

American Civil Liberties Union
3000 Connecticut Avenue N.W.
Washington, D.C.

Also helpful in any dealings with Congress is

The League of Women Voters
1730 M Street N.W.
Washington, D.C.

Senators represent far more people, and are able to give correspondingly less time to each. If the help you want is with a particular federal grant, project or agency, you are more likely to get help from a Representative than from a Senator. (Exception: small states with as many or more Senators than Representatives: Hawaii, Delaware, Vermont, Wyoming, etc. The bigger the population of a state, the more overworked the Senators.)

Sixth, Congressmen respect accurate information, careful organization, and effective follow-up action. If the first answer to your letter is not satisfactory, write a second. Many Congressmen will try to avoid taking firm positions on controversial issues. Don't let them. You are entitled to know how they vote in committee, how they actually feel about a bill, what they have done about your problem. When you ask a favor, make it specific, so you will know whether or not it was granted. And if it was, remember to thank your Congressman.

State Legislators

There are two major differences between Congress and most state legislatures. The first is that the average Congressman, who represents perhaps 500,000 people, has no personal knowledge of most of his constituents or their thoughts, while many a state assemblyman or senator may know key persons in virtually every neighborhood in his district. Second, the average state legislator has very limited access to staff and research facilities. While he is better equipped than the Congressman to know his people, he is less equipped to understand the issues.

The first way to get the word to a legislator is to plan your own legislative priorities far ahead; then you can suggest that a question on your issue be included on one of the questionnaires which many legislators send out to their constituents. This suggestion best originates from a key party official, someone who worked in a legislator's campaign, one of his staff members, or another member of the legislature. You ought to start work at least six months ahead of questionnaire time.

The second way is to talk to the people who influence the legislator before you talk with the legislator himself. Consult legislative assistants, key staff members to the legislature itself, officials of appropriate state departments or committees, officers of private groups in the field (say the local branch of the American Medical Association, hospital committee, and medical school on a health issue), your potential allies, and any of your past enemies that you think you might be able to bring along on this particular issue. The legislator will be more likely to listen to you if you can say that key citizens' groups in his own district support your proposal, as do other legislators with whom he works closely on other bills.

Because most legislators haven't enough staff to analyze all the issues involved in a legislative session, they tend to take a "Show me" attitude. You have to be able to document the need for specific changes in the status quo. If possible, have individual case histories of constituents available, showing the need for change. Pick case histories that even your opponents would feel uncomfortable about—particularly outrageous examples of how the status quo works out.

It is important to send written material before any meeting with a legislator so that you won't be put off with, "Well, let me read about this first." Open your interview with a statement about the material, implying that the legislator is now familiar with the positions it sets forth. Alternatively, if you are sure of getting two meetings, and have time, hand him your position paper at the first meeting and indicate your eagerness to discuss the issue further at the second interview.

Don't demand a commitment from your legislator too early. Politicians don't like to commit themselves until a situation has developed well enough for them to have seen and heard all interest groups involved. In any case, if you do get a public statement from your legislator, don't have him release it too soon; that gives the opposition something to shoot at. Remember that commitments on controversial issues are hardest to get just before an election. If you have to ask, try to find a vote in his record which is offensive to the groups who are supporting you, and convince him that his support of your issue is a

way to placate these people. If some of your supporters have been offended by an earlier vote, get them to write letters objecting to that vote, and asking his support for the issue you're working on now.

The Bureaucrat

The state legislature or Congress may set the broad policy rules for state and federal government. But the value of programs once they are launched depends on their implementation by the administrative agencies. The bureaucrat can make a population education program fly—or flop—without a mandate from the legislative branch; but he has a constant fear of that branch.

One of the first things a bureaucrat needs to know is how an idea will be received by key legislators—especially those who control his budget. Friendly support from the legislature can help remove the timidity and caution that characterize too many agencies.

But there still must be a positive motivation for change. You should know an agency's programs, as well as the mandate under which it carries them out, and you need to be able to point out any holes in those programs which your idea can fill neatly. You will thus be helping the agency to carry out its full mandate.

Bureaucrats dislike controversial issues, so try to find a way to present your proposal in as even-handed and un-threatening a way as possible. If you're trying to get a population education program set up in the schools, place great emphasis on the need for objectivity.

Try to demonstrate that the absence of such information in the curriculum makes the schools seem biased. Point out the possible political pitfalls of continuing with the status quo.

Agencies are accustomed to people trying to use them for their own selfish purposes. If you and your organization will not benefit directly from the proposal, say so. Emphasize that you are functioning as honest brokers, with no organizational stake in the program you are pushing. Try to find non-political, highly respectable persons who can actually develop the ideas for your program, once the concept is approved.

But the most forthright, well-documented and objective proposals may not move the bureaucracy. Don't be put off. You have a right to information, from federal agencies under the Freedom of Information Act, and in many states under similar statutes or judicial opinions.

Keep coming back after something is promised. If you get legal objections to your idea, bring your lawyer. And finally, remember that agencies are very jealous of their turf and may respond to quiet suggestions that if they don't move soon, someone else will clear up a problem. Don't be afraid. If worse comes to worst, indicate that you will hold the bureaucrat personally responsible for his action. The rule of the civil service is "Don't rock the boat," and the man whose house is picketed is often considered as responsible for boat-rocking as the picketers.

Develop contacts within the agency who

can feed you information about what is going on. Once you have contacts, protect them carefully. Let the supervisor know that you have information, but don't be too specific lest you compromise your source.

Industry and Advertising

Industry and advertising firms continue to promote their products and large families in the same breath, and you must convince them that the public accepts social norms other than large family size.

Letters can be powerful tools to accomplish this. A faithful program of writing, sustained over a reasonable period of time, will produce visible results.

The group most sensitive to adverse reaction is the advertising industry. If they find a large group of people responding unfavorably to an ad, they stop running it. National corporations have been known to change their advertising line in response to little more

OFFICE OF SENATOR BOB PACKWOOD

than a hundred letters.

Magazines are also responsive to indications of reader interest. In the last couple of years, many magazines have printed articles about population growth, birth control, sterilization and abortion, largely in response to letters from readers interested in these subjects. A few years ago these subjects were taboo.

The television industry is more difficult to influence than the magazine industry, because television is subject to closer government regulation and advertising pressure. Letter-writing to encourage serious coverage of population growth and related topics is important, but not decisive, in pushing for more intelligent coverage. Letter-writing campaigns are more persuasive when it comes to removing objectionable material from the airwaves. Serious, coherent, negative response to pronatalist material, especially in the fiction/game/soap-opera show area, can be most effective.

Universities and Other Nonprofit Organizations

The Chancellor of the University of California does not have much to do with the dean of a small women's college in the mid-South. About the only element common to most academic policy games is that while the politicking is often fierce, no one is willing to admit that it exists—and certainly no one wants to take the responsibility for it. Academic bureaucrats—or church officials, or the leaders of citizens' groups—prefer to duck

an issue or to pass it on. The hardest problem may be getting anyone to admit that he or she has the power to do anything about your grievance. It is important to have lots of facts in dealing with educational institutions; they need to have a thick file before they make a decision. If the offiicers complain that their hands are tied by the trustees, find a few trustees who agree with you and build up a storm. If you can't, threaten to influence the next election of trustees by campaigning, picketing or some other tactic. Above all, don't let the officers set up a study committee, unless they let you and your allies control it. Study committees are the graves of decisions.

When you are dealing with educational and other nonprofit organizations, remember that they see themselves as having limited purposes. Try to tie what you are doing to that official purpose. If you are against university policies which discriminate against women, gather evidence on how this hampers women's studies; if you are trying to get a resolution through an educational association, develop the best possible pedagogic arguments you can. Be specific on the links wherever possible, and, if the place is old, find what precedents and traditions are on your side as well as which ones are against you.

Chapter Five:
First Game: Faithful Ally

Now that you have organized your team and set up a training schedule, let's look at the rules of the game. Like any game, a policy contest has players, equipment (the resources), a definition of winning (the goal), and some rules and ideas about how to play (the strategies).

Notes on the Tax Laws

Before you can begin to play, however, you must have chips to play with—whether your games will be played on the floor of the legislature, in the courtroom or in the general election, consistent sources of money are necessary. Basically, money falls into two categories, depending upon the limitations placed on its use in policy games by the tax laws. *Hard money* is money given by an individual who does not want to take a tax deduction for giving it. It can be used for court suits, for direct lobbying and for supporting a political candidate. (If the money has been raised by or given directly to a corporation, it cannot be used in an election campaign, but it can be used for lobbying. This is the reason why political campaign committees are not corporate bodies, and, in fact, neither the Democratic nor the Republican National Committee is incorporated.)

Soft money is money originating with foundations, from universities and other nonprofit bodies, or given to tax-exempt organizations by individuals who do intend to take a tax deduction. Soft money cannot be used in political campaigns, nor can it be used "to influence the course of legislation." It can be used, of course, for educational activities; it can be used to fight court battles; and it can be used to influence administrative, as opposed to legislative, government bodies.

The kind of money your organization has will in some degree influence the kinds of games you can play, but remember that policy games are stacked in favor of the status quo, in favor of those we might call "insiders," in much the same way that the rules of black jack at a gambling casino are stacked in favor of the house. This does not mean that you, the outsider, can't win. It does mean that your first job is to ascertain the nature of the house advantage on any particular issue, and get around it.

Strategy

It is sometimes possible to break the bank; the 1973 Supreme Court decisions on abortion are a good example, in which the outsiders went in and just plain beat the system statutes. But this doesn't happen often. It is more effective, in most cases, to get help from some of the insiders. At a gambling casino, all the employees are working for the house, and there is careful supervision to insure that they don't form alliances with any of the players. Politics is a looser game. The dealers and croupiers are independent entrepreneurs trying to get ahead, and the key element in most winning strategies is to get some of them, at least, to work for change.

In order to do this, you need to figure out what it is about the status quo that appeals to the opposition, and how you can make change

If your organization has 501 (c) 3 status under the Internal Revenue code, it is tax-exempt, and contributions to it are also tax-exempt (such contributions are called "soft money"). Organizations with 501 (c) 3 status may

☐ appear at legislative hearings if invited to do so

☐ publish materials which will inform the public about a legislative issue as long as the materials take no stand on the issue

☐ publish records of candidates for election without endorsing a particular candidate

If your organization has 501 (c) 4 status it is tax-exempt, but contributions to it are not. Your organization

☐ may lobby directly

☐ may not participate in election campaigns

If your organization has no tax-exempt status, it may

☐ publish voting records

☐ endorse candidates

☐ work in political campaigns

☐ lobby directly

But if your organization is incorporated under the laws of any state, it may not contribute corporate funds to any political campaign.

Information on state regulations for registration of lobbyists can be obtained from the Secretary of State for your state, as can information about federal and state law regarding political fund-raising.

seem more attractive.

This is not easy; policy makers often conceal their real reasons for supporting the status quo. Assume the best—that it will be fairly easy to win the opposition over—and start with the easier games. If it turns out that you can't overcome the house advantage this way, move on to the more difficult games listed later in the chapter. Your team probably needs the practice with the simpler games, anyway. If you plunge headfirst into a major political campaign, and lose, your whole organization may go under. Try to build a winning record, and pick policy issues that can make you successful with your first targets. (You can still work on difficult issues.)

We call this game "the faithful ally." Imagine that you have a liberal church group, for instance, which favors programs of sex educa-

tion, but which doesn't do much to advance them because it is unwilling to assign its limited staff resources to do the job. Your strategy here is to go to them, offer your services as consultants, researchers, organizers or whatever is needed, and begin to work with them to build up their programs. There is only a small element of conflict: sex education is high on your priority list, and low on theirs. You might ultimately have been able to persuade them to change their priorities, but the easiest way to overcome the house advantage is to play alongside them.

Before you try to play faithful ally, however, you must have a cooperative policy maker who is basically sympathetic and who needs the resources you have to offer. To assess sympathy, look for leads in newspaper stories indicating that an official is interested

The game of faithful ally has often been combined with the idea of "education through experience." A good case study is a state government intern program offered by the Population Institute in Washington, D.C.

The intern program is designed to accelerate the development of state population policies and state population commissions. Sympathetic legislators are provided support for this by college student interns who, as part of their academic program, investigate population-related issues in state government. Graduate and undergraduate students work with legislators and other governmental officials in the state where they attend school. By making arrangements with a professor at their university, the students normally receive academic credit (equivalent to one course or more) for their reports. The Population Institute provides the interns with a small stipend and limited travel and research costs.

Each intern is encouraged to focus on a particular aspect of state population policy and to investigate, in depth, the way in which the state government has handled that issue. Topics of research include such issues as land-use planning, population and sex education, tax laws, abortion, family-planning services, etc.

One intern conducted a thorough survey of all legislation which affected fertility, directly or indirectly, in Michigan and provided her legislator with a summary of which laws should be changed to make contraceptives more available and effective. Two interns in Colorado provided their legislative advisors with a full summary of the various political factions involved in the land-use controversy in that state.

in the problem, in voting records kept by groups like ZPG, and in discussions with other individuals involved in population policy. Then you can usually follow up the lead with a phone call and a meeting.

Your ideas will get a good reception if you and your resources are valuable. If your target has very limited resources of its own, almost any help you can give will be welcomed. (Classically, state and local legislators are desperately short of staff for policy research, while administrative agencies are much better equipped.) The second way to show your value is to offer a resource the target is likely to lack. A large contraceptive manufacturer, for example, has lots of manpower, but he may lack access to the campus community for some of his educational/program materials. Or he may want advice on the best way to appeal to students. A corporation health service doesn't need volunteers to do its clerical work, but it may be totally unequipped to conduct a survey establishing the need for a corporation gynecologist.

In choosing a target, or an individual through whom to approach an institution, don't ignore personality factors. Caesar wanted "men about me that are sleek and fat," without Cassius' "lean and hungry look." But Caesar spoke for the status quo, and you, we assume, seek change. That means it is the lean and hungry people, the ambitious ones, the empire builders, that you need to seek out. It is much more effective to do a good piece of policy development and bill writing for a powerful committee chairman or an aggressive legislator than for an earnest, sincere but ineffectual legislator who is likely to lose his next election. Remember, as an ally, you not only are interested in how deeply your target wants *you*, but in how badly you want *him*.

In dealing with administrative agencies or universities, be especially careful. Real power relationships in such institutions often belie the organizational chart. Try to pick someone who badly needs your help and can be helpful in return. Remember, great alliances are built on nothing more elevated than back scratching.

Tactics and Rules of the Game

If you have an organization with a fairly large number of supporters, you can offer to do a large part of your ally's scout-work for him. The classic model of a policy situation dependent upon great quantities of volunteers is a political campaign, and the lower the level, the more important the volunteers.

If you are going to use your manpower in a political campaign, remember a few rules. First, the campaign organizers call the shots. Nothing is less valued than volunteer labor that "does its own thing." Second, make sure your identification is clear, and that you get credit for what you do. Have your volunteers man the phone banks on a particular evening or evenings; have them wear their identifying buttons if they are working in the back rooms where the public won't see them.

If the candidate is successful, this kind of campaign alliance can be turned into a valuable and permanent working relationship with an important public official. If it's done well, it has as high a pay-off as almost any

other use of low-level volunteer labor.

Other possible forums for this tactic are petitions and initiative drives to conduct surveys and gather information, to picket, or to hand out leaflets of an organization with which you are allied. It is important that the workers who volunteer get a sense of accomplishment out of the effort. Socializing is probably most important in this kind of activity, which can be isolating and discouraging if there is no positive feedback.

Staff Assistance

Policy makers, whether in government, industry or education, are, by the very nature of their jobs, generalists. It is a rare legislator, corporation executive or academic administrator who knows enough facts about population or environmental issues to fill a two-page book. State and federal legislators are called upon to make decisions in a wide variety of areas in which they have no expertise. To a lesser extent, this is true of policy makers in the private sector.

As a result, the person who can provide expertise or arrange a liaison between the administrator and the expert is viewed as a valuable asset—provided the policy maker doesn't fear exploitation by the expert or is not hostile to the content of his message.

In the various areas of population policy which have been referred to previously, students can successfully play the role of staff assistant for population matters. This is certainly the case wth Population Institute interns, who carry out research on legislative

issues concerned with population. Similarly, the ZPG lobbyists in Washington are called upon frequently to provide population information to Congressmen—and they sometimes have written speeches for them on this issue.

Similar services can be provided to any type of policy maker who is already or potentially an ally. Students, for instance, could consider contacting contraceptive manufacturers to offer assistance in research or advice on improvement of contraceptive distribution in their area—or they might actually sell contraceptives. One way to keep a supply of spending money is to offer condoms or other non-prescription contraceptives for sale in a volunteer's dorm. More than one student has successfully operated such a business—buying condoms wholesale, and marking the price up slightly before sale. The price is still far below those of the neighborhood pharmacies, and the supply is convenient since it is right on campus.

Another way you can work as an ally on population issues is as an aid to a government agency—especially if you live in or near the

state capital. Very often such agencies are concerned with population issues, but lack the staff to acquire data on which to base decisions. Likely candidates for such assistance are the departments of education, health, planning, welfare, natural resources, etc. The administrator in the department will often welcome an offer for a survey in such areas as the content of sex education in the schools, availability of contraceptive information and services to minors or to the poor, the attitudes of county commissioners toward regional land-use planning, etc.

If you are a student, you can insure sufficient time for such activities by requesting that you receive academic credit for your research. Usually, the easiest way to do this is to arrange for an independent study course with one faculty member to oversee the scope of the project. In some cases, an entire class in environmental studies has participated in this type of survey, with each student submitting a summary of findings and experiences as a term paper.

If a student is lucky enough to be in a

Population Information Libraries

You will be a more reliable ally if you are accurate. Population libraries are helpful in this respect. The best key to collections and services around the country and world is *International Directory of Population Information and Library Resources* ($7.00), available from the Technical Information Programs, Carolina Population Center, University Square, Chapel Hill, North Carolina 27514. Many libraries offer free bibliographies, acquisitions lists and reference services. Unless otherwise noted, these libraries have general population collections:

California Institute of Technology, Caltech Population Program Library, Pasadena, California

Cornell University, International Population Program Research Library, Ithaca, New York

Florida State University, Population Studies Program, Tallahasse, Florida

Harvard University, Harvard Center for Population Studies Library, Cambridge, Massachusetts (they will send bibliographies)

University of Hawaii, East-West Population Institute Reference Collection, Honolulu, Hawaii

Johns Hopkins University, Department of Population Dynamics Library, Baltimore, Maryland

Miami University, Scripps Foundation for Research in Population Problems, Oxford, Ohio

University of Michigan, Center for Population Planning, Ann Arbor, Michigan

University of North Carolina, Carolina Population Center Library, Chapel Hill, North Carolina

University of Pennsylvania (demography, statistics), Population Studies Center, Philadelphia, Pennsylvania

Princeton University (Demographical / Statistical / Family Planning Collection), Office of Population Research, Princeton, New Jersey

University of Texas at Austin, Population Research Center, Austin, Texas

Tufts University, Fletcher School of Law and Diplomacy (population policy collection), Medford, Massachusetts

school with a population study center, he or she can often become the informal link between the center and a governmental agency or legislator. Population centers are usually more than happy to cooperate with students who are working to see that the expertise on hand is heard and utilized by policy makers.

Another way you can play faithful ally is to act as a ghost-writer. Most speeches on population issues are not written by the prominent public figures who deliver them, but by people who have the necessary time and

---

Population/Family Planning Organizations

If you need information on any aspect of population action, population resource centers around the country are there to help you. Contact any of the following:

Planned Parenthood/Washington Office at 1666 K St., N.W., Suite 91, Washington, D.C. 20006. Provides information on state and federal policy development; publishes *Family Planning/Population Reporter* (free); provides copies of state legislation for 75 cents each.

Planned Parenthood–World Population, McCormick Library, 810 Seventh Ave., New York, N. Y. 10019. Publishes periodic bibliographies, annotated acquisitions lists (free); has limited reference library, copying equipment; provides reprints of *Family Planning Perspectives*.

Planned Parenthood resource centers in Chicago, Seattle, Baltimore, and Austin contain small libraries and media collections.

The Population Council, 245 Park Ave., New York, N. Y. 10017. General population library, international in orientation; supplies bibliographies (free); does reference work. Population Council's Information Office brings new information to atten-

tion of U.S. policy makers, publishes professional materials (free) in international family planning-related areas.

Population Reference Bureau, 1755 Massachusetts Ave., N.W., Washington, D.C. 20036. Set of publications which provide good reference materials for teachers and students in general population studies; library publishes acquisitions lists and answers specific reference questions.

SIECUS (Sex Information and Education Council of the U.S.), 1855 Broadway, New York, N. Y. 10023. Provides bibliographies, reading lists (free); has several publications; will answer specific inquiries about sex education policies and programs.

Zero Population Growth, 1346 Connecticut Ave., N.W., Washington, D.C. 20036. Sends members the *National Reporter*, which gives up-to-date information on federal legislation and action items, and *Equilibrium*, reporting in depth on issues; has a very active group working to change pronatalist statements appearing in advertising, the media, and other areas; *Population Policy Platform*; rating charts of U.S. Senators and Representatives; checklist of local growth issues; etc. Membership is $15.00, $8.00 for students.

---

knowledge. It takes a long time for an alliance to get to the stage where a legislator will trust you with speech writing. But there are many other important drafting tasks you can assume earlier in your alliance.

One such task is initial preparation of legislation. Often, constituent groups take prepared bills to a state legislator for his use. Some legislators have a tradition that any bill which a constituent requests will be introduced "by request." It is better, however, even

if your state has that tradition, to get the legislator to adopt your idea as his own. A checklist of model state legislation can be obtained from ZPG National. Individual copies of state bills can be obtained for a small fee from the Washington office of national Planned Parenthood.

In playing a staff role, try to keep your agenda and that of your ally separate in your mind. If you are drafting something for him, and want it to be used, make sure that it re-

---

Internship Groups

More than twenty-five state governments have legislative and/or administrative state internship programs. A list of these is available from the Council of State Governments (Ironworks Pike, Spindletop, Lexington, Kentucky 40505).

Other programs in which an intern could work in population-related areas include:

OXFAM-America, Room 922, 1028 Connecticut Ave., N.W., Washington, D.C. 20036. Flexible program based on development-population research project; OXFAM staff works with student interns, partially in Washington.

Student Intern Program, Summer Institute in Clinical Legal Education, University of Denver College of Law, Denver, Colo. 80210. Credit work for first-year law students; internships in Denver in areas of legislation, counseling and community work; environmental Internship and Community Renewal Development. (There are similar clinical programs at most law schools.)

Population Institute Student Intern Program, 110 Maryland Ave., N.E., Washington, D.C. 20002. Academic credit, stipends and travel expenses for undergraduate and graduate students working in the states where they study. Students work with legistlators, state agencies and public interest groups on issues relating to population, land use and environment.

For information concerning U.N. internships, some of which are population-oriented, write: International Directory for Youth Internships at the United Nations, Its Specialized Agencies and Non-Governmental Organizations, c/o U.S. Committee for UNICEF, 331 East 33rd St., New York, N. Y. 10016.

---

flects any concrete ideas he already has. The place to influence him is in the broad area where he is likely not to have any clear position. Explain to him not only the arguments for the position you are selling him, but also the arguments against. Nothing sours an alliance faster than for one ally to find himself out on a limb where he has been placed by another.

If you put a controversial point in a floor statement for a legislator, make sure he knows how to defend it, and that it *is* controversial. If you make a statement in a letter to a state agency from someone prominent, make sure it is correct and that you can document it. Accuracy is the essence of a good staff relationship. Your reputation for accuracy and frankness, or sloppiness and unreliability, will spread much faster than your message about population.

Chapter Six:
Second Game:
The Mandarin Elite

Playing the faithful ally will only carry you so far. Eventually, you must cope with those who are not ready to support you, even if you put in your resources. This brings us to another of our policy games, called "the mandarin elite." This game can be helpful when the major obstacle to developing a new policy is that it lacks intellectual respectability. The basic strategy of "the mandarin elite" is to make *your* ideas, not those of the established order, the intellectually respectable ones. This is a matter partly of good argument, and partly of *who* makes the argument and *where*.

Strategy: Making New Ideas Intellectually Respectable

The problem of intellectual legitimization is particularly important when dealing with universities, boards of education and non-profit organizations, which don't like to admit that they play the policy game. They are most likely to respond to an initiative sponsored by one of their professional peers. For example, in 1972, various population groups wanted the prestigious American Association for the Advancement of Science to pass a resolution supporting the renewal of federal family-planning legislation. The resolution was drafted by staff members of an activist population organization, and it was sponsored by a prominent scientist. AAAS officials might never have supported the group's resolution without the endorsement of the scientist.

A ZPG chapter at Yale University was in-strumental in convincing the university administration to include demography in the undergraduate curriculum—this at a time when the university staff was being reduced in response to the severe financial squeeze of 1969–1970. The way the ZPG chapter managed this seemingly impossible feat was to go to the heads of several academic departments —including history, sociology, public health, forestry, biology, urban studies, and economics—all of whom stated that having a demographer on the staff of the university was very important to their own departments. Response was slow in coming, but within a year and a half, a part-time appointment was arranged for a demographer to help lead a blue-ribbon multidisciplinary seminar course on environmental studies. In addition, the Sociology Department appointed a full-time assistant professor in demography.

When it comes to politics, this kind of intellectual stamp of approval is likely to be more important in dealing with legislative committees than in persuading individual legislators, since the committees generally have had the responsibility for developing the established approach, and thus have a stronger vested interest in it. Usually, too, it helps if your program is supported by academics from *your* state university. It may even matter which state college speaks out, since some legislative committees have traditionally nurtured a close relationship with particular branches of the state university or particular private colleges. (Always check on the *alma mater* of a person you want to influence.)

Case Study: Palo Alto Land Development

The mandarin elite game, played well, can have astonishing results. The city of Palo Alto, California, was faced with a choice of alternate development patterns for an area called the Foothills which lay at the edge of the city limits. There was already considerable sentiment against growth in the Palo Alto area, and the opposition was able to prevail upon the city to commission a $144,000 study by a city planning firm.

The City Council asked the firm to analyze the area's ecology, geology, climate, vegetation, soils, mineral resources, utilities, trafficways, recreation needs, transit; it asked the firm to develop twenty possible land-use patterns for The Foothills, and requested figures on the suitability of various sub-areas for development.

When all the costs and revenues to the city had been estimated, the findings showed that there was no development pattern that did not result in a net cost to the taxpayers of Palo Alto over a twenty-year period. It even turned out that it was cheaper and more advantageous to purchase the 6,100 acres of land for $30,000,000 over a thirty-year period than to permit it to be developed. The study further found that, after the twenty-year period, the costs to the taxpayers of having this 6,100 acres developed would continue to increase, while after the thirty-year bonds were paid off, the costs of keeping the land open would be minimal. The study recommended that the bulk of the Foothills area be left as permanent open space in a bi-county regional park district.

This study completely altered the dimensions of the local growth debate in the Palo Alto area. The proposals of the firm were submitted to the voters, who approved them—and an idea which would have seemed totally unsound without the evidence garnered by the survey was enthusiastically adopted because it had been endorsed by the mandarin elite.

Tactics

In playing the mandarin elite game, it is fatal to assume that the day will be carried by your conviction that the proposal is urgently needed. Right seldom constitutes might in the world of policy. No public decision-maker will advocate untried programs without heavy and respectable support, and any strategy that assumes he will is doomed to the attic room of "lunatic causes."

Creating the appearance of broad support for a proposal is not unlike selling men's hair spray to the millions of males watching Sunday afternoon football on TV. Providing "respectability" is the first step in establishing anything new in a mass market. To be accepted, a new product or proposal must appear non-controversial and, above all, safe. Therefore, endorsements from "respectable" and reassuring sources represent a good opening gambit.

Just as testimonials from Truman Capote and Alice Cooper would do little to quell the fear of sexually insecure males about the "dry look," endorsements from Abbie Hoffman and Mick Jagger for the provision of contraceptives to minors would hardly convince older Americans that this is a cause whose time finally has come.

A good rule of thumb in seeking endorsements is to go after individuals and representatives of organizations who are considered wedded to the status quo on most issues and, therefore, are assumed to be against the proposal they subsequently endorse. Obviously, the most effective endorsement of a proposal to disseminate contraceptives to adolescents would be from the Pope. Failing that, Billy Graham and Shirley Temple Black might be best—despite the fact that they have no special knowledge of the problem. After all, "respectability" and expertise have never been really correlated in the public mind.

Obtaining the endorsements of "respectable" people is not as difficult as it might appear. For better or worse, most of us in the population-environment movement are college-educated and came from middle-income and upper-middle-income families. Many of us have inherited contacts, through relatives and acquaintances, with people like the president of the state bar association, the director of a local hospital, a prominent judge, a renowned academician, a popular athlete, or virtually anyone of "standing" in the community. Nationally-known "respectables" are best reached through national organizations which share an interest in the proposal to be endorsed, such as labor unions, professional organizations and Washington-based public interest groups.

Always approach a potential endorser with a final copy of the statement to be endorsed. Few people will lend their names to only a verbal approximation or rough draft of a statement for ultimate release.

Another way to legitimatize an idea is through print and electronic media, since in some sense it is true that an idea does not seem real to people until they begin to read or hear about it. The proper approach to such media legitimization depends on the nature of your idea. It is important here to distinguish between the kind of coverage which makes an idea respectable, and the kind which identifies the supporters of an idea. A scholarly journal does the former, but little else. A demonstration does the latter, but little else. A report on a paper delivered at the annual meeting of a fairly influential local organization may do both. So, before you go after the press, decide which goal is more important to you.

In trying to legitimize an idea with a particular target, you have to begin with the medium which reaches that target. Usually this means a special channel, rather than general mass-circulation papers, unless you are dealing with the whole population. University administrators, government officials in a particular department, industry officials—all these have certain publications, certain conferences, certain newsletters, which they rely heavily upon. You can get this kind of information from friendly sources who are in the same profession.

Then you have to figure out how you can get your message into that channel. Papers and speeches are among the best message carriers; they are usually newsworthy, they clearly identify a prestigious sponsor (the speaker) as well as a forum (the conference) and are fairly easy to arrange. Often all you need to do is find out who is scheduled to speak at the next meeting of a key group, and go to him with a careful presentation of your idea.

Once you arrange to have an idea surface, you need to see that it is covered. Here the key instruments are the press release and the press conference. The easiest way of learning how to put these together is to use another organization's press release or press conference as a model. Pick the brains of the person who wrote or organized it. Other possible sources of good advice are newspaper reporters who are known to be friendly. Journalism students at a university often will welcome the chance to put their skills to real use. You might also receive help from other organizations in the environmental and population field.

Don't try to have a press conference without such help, unless you really cannot get it. Seemingly small details about scheduling time (will it make deadlines?), day of the week (when are the favorable reporters likely to be available?), place, and wording of your release, will make an immense difference in the coverage you get.

So get professional advice. ZPG National can send you a press kit, but it cannot give you the local specifics you need.

State and National Population Commissions

Population commissions provide a highly visible means of exploring alternative mechanisms and goals for population policy and for collecting relevant data. The very existence of these commissions gives legitimacy to the idea of concrete population action. Hawaii, California, Colorado, Massachusetts and Michigan, among other states, have had special legislative committees dealing with population growth and distribution. Legislation for the establishment of population commissions has been introduced in Michigan, California and Wisconsin, and has been enacted in Hawaii, Colorado and Massachusetts. Model legislation for population commissions is available for 75 cents from Planned Parenthood, Washington Office, 1666 K Street, N.W., Washington, D.C. 20006.

The research done for the Commission on Population Growth and the American Future —much of it premier investigation in policy areas—is available from the Government Printing Office at $4.25 for each volume. Volume IV (*Government and Population*), Volume V (*Population Distribution and Policy*), and Volume VI (*Aspects of Population Growth Policy*) are most relevant to policy issues.

Religious Groups and Church Committees

Religious groups and population committees in churches have been most active in supporting sex education programs, supporting or fighting abortion reform, and dealing with environmental issues; you'll find that when it comes to making an idea respectable, they are as helpful as anyone. Among these, the Catholic church and the Unitarian church have perhaps the most comprehensive curricula in sex education. The Department of Population Problems within the United Methodist Church (100 Maryland Avenue, N.E., Washington, D.C. 20002) is the largest church office actively working with popula-

tion affairs. The department works within the church and community at large to disseminate information about population issues and develop support for early stabilization of population size.

Legal, Scientific, Professional Bodies

Many learned bodies and professional groups have population-related departments which are good sources of ammunition, and which may sometimes be prevailed on to come to the support of your program.

The American Bar Association has a Committee on Overpopulation and the Law and a Family Planning Committee which has endorsed the Uniform Abortion Act. For more information about these groups, contact the ABA, Office of Information, 1155 East 60th Street, Chicago, Ill. 60637.

The American Medical Association has a Committee on Maternal and Child Health within its Department of Environmental, Public and Occupational Health which, in recent years, has liberalized its stand on contraceptive services to minors and the need for parental/spouse consent. For information about AMA policies and activities, contact AMA (Policies and Activities), 535 North Dearborn Street, Chicago, Ill. 60610, or the Center for the Advancement of Population Studies in Medicine, 49 Delsar Street, Buffalo, N.Y. 14216.

The Population Association of America (Box 14182, Benjamin Franklin Station, Washington, D.C. 20044) is an organization for professionals in population, emphasizing

demographic research. It publishes the journal *Demography* ($20.00 a year), the periodic annotated bibliography *Population Index*, and *PAA Affairs*, a quarterly newsletter ($2.00 per year). Membership, including subscriptions to all three of the above, costs $6.00 per year for students. These materials will probably be helpful for those who want intellectual depth in population; however, they contain only a slight emphasis on policy.

The American Public Health Association has a Population Committee which has taken good positions on population issues. It's address is APHA, 1015 18th Street, N.W., Washington, D.C. 20036.

University Population Centers

There are more than forty population centers and departments in, or affiliated with, U.S. universities and colleges. Most of these have significant policy research and policy courses. A few of the larger population centers which offer concentrations in policy are: University of California at Berkeley (International Population and Urban Research); Cornell University (International Population Program); Duke University (Population Studies Program); Fletcher School of Law and Diplomacy at Harvard and Tufts (Law and Population Program); Harvard (Center for Population Studies); University of Hawaii (East-West Population Institute and the International Health/Population and Family Planning Program); University of Michigan (Department of Population Planning and the Population Studies Center);

Basic Bibliography on Legitimatizing Key Policy Issues

POPULATION COMMISSIONS: *The Report of the Commission on Population Growth and the American Future*, available at many bookstores or from the Government Printing Office, Superintendent of Documents, Washington, D.C. 20402. ($1.75)

"Legal Obstacles to Freedom of Choice in the Areas of Contraception, Abortion, and Voluntary Sterilization in the United States," *Aspects of Population Growth Policy*, The Report of the Commission on Population Growth and the American Future, Volume 6. Government Printing Office, Washington, D.C. 20402.

FAMILY PLANNING SERVICES: "The Health and Social Consequences of Teenage Childbearing" by Jane Menchen from *Family Planning Perspectives*, Vol. 4, #3, July, 1972. PP-WP, Information and Education Office, 810 Seventh Avenue, New York, N. Y. 10019. (35¢)

ABORTION: The Supreme Court Decision on Abortion: Roe, et al., v. Wade, District Attorney of Dallas County (No. 70-18) and Doe et al., v. Bolton, Attorney General of Georgia et al. (No. 70-40). Government Printing Office.

"Resolutions on Abortion Adopted by Churches and Other Organizations." Includes statements by AMA, twelve protestant dominations, various Jewish bodies and the Unitarian-Universalist Association. The Department of Population Problems, United Methodist Church, 100 Maryland Avenue, N.E., Washington, D.C. 20002. ($2.00)

POPULATION AND FAMILY LIFE AND SEX EDUCATION: "Statements by Catholic Bishops concerning Sex Education" and "Interfaith Statements on Sex Education." Family Life Bureau/ U.S. Catholic Conference, 1312 Massachusetts Avenue, N.W., Washington, D.C. 20005.

Sex Code of California: A Compendium. 1973. Compendium of laws with a good bibliography and glossary. Public Education and Research Committee of California: 1760 Berkeley, Calif. 94707.

LAND-USE LAWS: *Quiet Revolution in Land-Use Control* (Dec. 1971). Offers good run-down on states with land-use legislation. The Council on Environmental Quality, 722 Jackson Place, N.W., Washington, D.C. 20006. Summary 45 cents, entire report $1.26.

National Land-Use Legislation: Monograph #4. Monograph on model legislation. American Law Institute, 4025 Chestnut Street, Philadelphia, Pa. 19104. ($4.25)

University of North Carolina, Chapel Hill (Carolina Population Center); University of Wisconsin, Madison (Center for Demography and Ecology), etc.

For a more complete list of centers, with addresses, ask for the *Directory of Population Research and Study Centers in the U.S.A.* (free), published yearly by Planned Parenthood-World Population, McCormick Library, 810 Seventh Avenue, New York, N.Y. 10019. For an even more complete list of population study centers, with careful (if somewhat dated) descriptions, write for the *Directory of Population Study Centers*, from the Population Association of America, P.O. Box 14182, Benjamin Franklin Station, Washington, D.C. 20024.

Chapter Seven:
Third Game:
People's Will

The will of the people can be effective against almost any target. Even industry is susceptible to pressure from large numbers of customers and potential customers. It's better, and easier, if you can select an audience a little more specific than "voters" or "customers." It might take 10,000 protesting letters to a company about their advertising program to make a dent, but 200 complaints from dealers about complaining customers could have the same effect. Likewise, in dealing with administrative agencies, a letter of complaint from a legislator is worth many times more than the same letter from a private citizen. (And, of course, one letter from the governor probably has the same effect as twenty from the legislature.)

But in lobbying efforts, the most common form of the game we'll call "the people's will," some pressure of numbers from ordinary citizens is needed to make the point, though contacts from prominent types are still valuable.

The key to a successful letter-writing campaign is organization. Few issues have so little public support that there actually aren't enough citizens willing to write, and if by chance you hit upon such an issue, you have no business following it up. But most public sentiment on political issues remains inert, and your job is to energize that part which is on your side.

If you plan to play the people's will game on a number of issues, your first step should be to build up a core of regular letter writers. These can be people who are interested in population issues, but who don't like meetings or cannot come to them. For more information on how to help your members write effective letters, write ZPG National. (Address on page 33.)

From time to time, issues come up on which you want to generate mail from many more people than your regular supporters. The best way to do this is to go to a meeting where you expect a large concentration of supporters of your ideas. Take a flyer which describes your issue and indicates the reasons why letters are needed. Do not provide a sample letter, as people will copy it, and such form letters usually do not count for much with politicians. Do supply paper, pens, envelopes and stamps.

On issues of fairly broad interest, you can even try to set up letter-writing tables in public places such as shopping centers, though there are problems in doing this. (See paragraph below on petitions.) If you want to insure a steady flow of mail, rather than a great rush, provide people with blank envelopes at the table, collect the envelopes and then mail them yourself when you want to. Assure interested people that handwritten, short notes are fine, but postcards are worth much less.

Your regular supporters should be urged to write on their business stationery if they have it, particularly if they are members of the professions or work for large organizations.

More detailed information on the whys and hows of good letters can be obtained in a pamphlet available from the League of Women Voters in your city. The Chamber of Commerce also puts out a sheet describing how to write good letters to legislators.

Letters, then, provide the sense of numbers which is critical to successfully playing the game of people's will. They can be supplemented when a measure is coming up for a crucial vote or faces the possibility of a veto, by public opinion telegrams—which cost less than $1.00 for 25 words—or by telephone calls in support of your position. A telephone tree is helpful in coordinating the phone calls.

Direct visits by your supporters to politicians add weight to your position. Even U.S. Congressmen are not as difficult to see as most constituents imagine, especially in Washington, and most state senators and representatives are quite accessible. It is very difficult for the politician to evade a question when he is asked directly by a constituent, whereas it is easy to answer a letter in a plausible way that commits the author to nothing. So encourage your most activist members to pay visits to their representatives whenever an important issue is under debate.

In some states, the constitution permits citizens to petition a law directly onto the ballot for decision by the voters. This kind of petition is an *initiative* procedure, and much more effective than a petition which merely calls on a legislator to vote a particular way. In trying to use it, you need to keep in mind its rather special purposes: it is likely to be valuable only where the proposed bill is fairly easy to explain to the voters, where the bill is likely to have widespread appeal, and where it cannot be passed in the legislature because of the opposition of entrenched, but minority, interests. The defeat of abortion referenda in California in 1970 and in 1972, and of environmental referenda in California in 1970 and 1972, are warnings: the fact that public opinion polls show public support does not tell you whether that support will stand up against a well-financed PR smear campaign.

Initiative measures must be drafted very carefully, preferably in consultation with legislative draftsmen who have worked with the legislature, and certainly with a good lawyer. Several environmental initiatives have been defeated because of sloppy draftsmanship, and others, successful at the polls, were invalidated by the courts.

The other major problem is getting your initiative qualified for the ballot in the first place. Shopping centers are clearly the best places to get signatures—indeed, virtually the only places with enough traffic to make setting up tables worthwhile. However, a recent Supreme Court ruling holds that shopping center owners, if they choose, may exclude persons seeking to circulate petitions, unless the petition is directly related to the center and for this reason cannot be circulated elsewhere. Union pickets, for example, cannot be excluded from the parking lot, but petitioners for an Equal Rights Amendment to the state constitution can be, because they could, in theory, circulate their petition elsewhere to achieve their goal.

However, many states do have legislation

which protects the right of access for initiatives. If your state is among them, you should come prepared to withstand harassment. First, check with the local police, inform them of your schedule, and try to get them on your side—or at least to acknowledge your rights. Thereafter, in many cases, a simple phone call from you to the manager of the shopping center will smooth your path. Sometimes, however, you will no sooner have set up your table than the mall manager, uniformed guard, or passers-by will begin telling you that "this is private property," or that "you've been asked to leave or we'll call the police." Remain calm, bring out a copy of the relevant legal citations (prepared by an attorney), and state that you are aware of your rights and are prepared to sue for false arrest.

If a shopping center guard threatens to evict you bodily himself, ask him if he is a police officer with arrest powers. Ask for proof.

Even if you manage to gather the signatures, various government officials are likely to play the "invalid signature" game. The largest number of invalid signatures in most petition drives result from an "incorrect" address beside the signature. This happens when someone moves and neglects to change his voter registration address. He puts down his current address, but it does not match the registration book. The only way to cope with this is to ask each petitioner two questions before he or she signs: "Are you registered?" and "What is the address at which you registered?" Those who are not registered must

register before they sign your petition; those who wish to change their registration can be supplied with a "change of registration" card by the petitioner.

You also should obtain, from the County Registrar, a written statement as to what he considers to be a valid signature; Registrars often have considerable leeway in deciding what the requirements are. Make sure that each signature complies with this local guideline.

If this sounds like a lot of work, it is; initiatives are hard work, but sometimes can be the only way to prove public support, even if they don't succeed the first time around.

LET'S MAKE

LiNDSaY

LINDSAY
FOR PRESIDENT

Chapter Eight:
Fourth Game:
David and Goliath

There comes a time in every political movement when, by all reasonable measures, the policy makers should be playing the game by your rules—but aren't. You may have provided them with all the staff assistance they need, flooded their hearing rooms with the nation's leading scientists to speak for your proposal, and demonstrated by opinion polls that two-thirds of the public supports you. But inertia, tradition and, most important, the effective policy gamesmanship of the opposition, are still hindering you. Perhaps, as with the Equal Rights Amendment, the major obstacle is simply that most of the people with power would lose some of their power by approving.

Strategy: Shifting the Balance of Power

This is a situation in which you have to decide to play David and Goliath: to actually go out and take power away from those who have it; to replace one policy maker with another of your choice; to shift policy arenas; to go to the courts to declare a statute unconstitutional, to the legislature to compel a state agency to mend its ways, to the stockholders to change management attitudes in the corporation, to the voters to get you or your candidate elected.

In playing David and Goliath, you are very likely to lose the first time around. So, don't try at all unless you are committed to trying several times, and have the resources.

Suppose you are in a situation where there is no choice but to play David and Goliath. It is important to pick your weapons carefully;

David did not go out to wrestle Goliath—he used a sling. The direct approach often is not the best. For example, if you find yourself in a situation where the state legislature simply refuses to move on a contraception bill because of heavy pressure from opponents, you may try to shift the focus of the battle to the courts, where the number of constituents may count less. This, in essence, was the strategy which, in many states, finally succeeded in removing restrictive abortion statutes from the books.

If the governor of your state is hostile to a program you support, you can resort to the help of your friends in the legislature. If, for instance, he has instructed the state's education department not to engage in a program of population education or sex education, the legislature can pass a bill instructing it to do so. If he refuses to act on sex discrimination against women in state employment, the legislature can create an independent commission to fight the bias.

Another indirect way of playing David and Goliath is to elevate a state battle to the federal level. Again, this happened on the abortion issue where, in addition to a number of favorable decisions from state courts, the final and critical opinion came from the U.S. Supreme Court. States began passing good legislation relating to women's rights about the time that the U.S. Congress passed and sent to the states the Equal Rights Amendment.

If your state government is reluctant to fund a particular program, try to find a federal bureau that is willing to put up the money. If the state health department refuses to set up family planning or sterilization clinics, you may be able to get federal funding for a private effort in the area.

You will note that we are suggesting that you try everything before you risk an all-out, direct battle: the very fact that you have to resort to such a battle normally means that there is a good chance you will lose. And once you lose such a direct battle, many of the indirect strategies become impossible, because potential allies are afraid to align themselves on the losing side.

Forming and Using Alliances

Before you launch a real battle, it is important to build as strong a network of alliances as possible—and it is necessary to maintain that network during your battle. There are a number of pitfalls to beware of in dealing with your allies.

First, remember that more political alliances are probably founded on ego issues than any other single factor. The easiest way to deal with this is to create a "non-group," a coalition of all the groups. Specify that, after this one battle, the coalition will cease to exist, and then let the coalition call the meetings, issue the press releases, etc. This way, no one worries unduly about the fact that a future competitor for press, money and members is getting an unfair share of the glory.

Second, if you set up a coalition for one purpose, stick to that purpose, and that purpose only. If you load a large number of potentially divisive issues on a coalition, you reduce its potential base of support.

Coalitions and alliances require regular meetings of their steering committees; but try not to make these meetings a setting for egotistical parliamentary games. Don't be afraid to vote on an issue, however often it turns out that what appear to be serious disagreements are not real at all.

Your coalition will need someone to take on the staff work of holding it together, someone who is not fully committed to the organizational work of one of the individual allies. The strength of your alliance will also be cemented by clear assignments of tasks to members. Don't be afraid to ask your allies to do particular tasks, but see that the tasks concern their specialties, and not yours. The more that individual allies have put into a common effort, the less likely they are to walk out over trivia.

And, like your organization, your alliance needs symbolic victories.

Winning in the Legislature: Headcounts, Swingvotes, Parliamentary Strategy

If your alliance is trying to get legislative action, as opposed to electoral or judicial action, it will probably have to take responsibility for a good deal of the "internal" intelligence for the final roll calling, putting out legislative announcements, and making sure that legislators show for the vote. Because many population issues are relatively nonpartisan, your allies in the legislature may not have access to head counts.

The first thing you need for an all-out legislative battle is a head count. You should

begin very early to determine the probable position of every legislator, and categorize him as for you, against you or a swing vote. Many of the swing votes have made up their minds but are not revealing it. You want to keep enough grass-roots voter pressure on the legislators to insure that they stay on your side, but—most important—you want to get them to restate their positions publicly, in a number of different contexts. Ideally, get the legislator to make a speech on the subject, or convince a few others of his constituents to vote your way. All these acts tie him into his position, and minimize his freedom to switch.

The one exception to these rules is on issues of extraordinary emotional impact, like abortion. There, a legislator may make it clear to you that he will vote, but only if his position is not publicized, because he is afraid of the pressure that will build up. In this case, honor his wishes.

The swing vote is your major target. This is where to focus the greater part of your energy; this is where to aim your letters and visits. If the other side is better organized than you are, you may want to go to the swing voter early and ask him to promise not to make a public commitment until you have had a chance to talk to him.

The legislator who tells you he is against your position will probably vote that way, and it may not be worth your time and energy to try to bring him around. But if his present position is inconsistent with his constituency or his past record, you might try to win him over—always trying to keep his present position off the public record. (The opposition, of course, is simultaneously trying to put him on the record.)

When you are counting potential votes, remember that those who side with you are more likely to tell you their position than those who do not: don't feel confident merely because two-thirds of those whose position you know are on your side, if half the total votes are listed as "unknown." (If half are unknown, you should be running at least three to one in your own count.)

Just having votes, of course, is not enough. The voters have to show up on the crucial day. The specific arrangement you should make to "whip" your votes to the legislative floor varies from state to state. Consult your experienced lobbyist, the League of Women Voters, an environmental group or a trade union for tips. You probably will want to combine a phone bank to reach all offices with visits by constituents to anyone who may try to "take a walk" and not vote on the issue.

Once the legislators are on the floor, there are numerous parliamentary tactics that can influence the outcome of the vote. Few outsiders are knowledgeable on such matters. The most you can hope for is to see that one of the leaders of your side within the legislature is known for parliamentary cunning. Important indicators of how your proposal will do are the amount of committee time alloted for its debate, the order in which amendments are taken up, the day of the week, and the point in the legislative session in which the proposal will be voted on.

Once a bill is successfully through the legislature, of course, it usually requires the signature of the governor or President. This final hurdle may be easy or very tough, but the tactics used to overcome it are straightforward: lots of pressure from people the governor cares about. Population issues are controversial enough that you are not likely to be able to override a governor's veto on the floor—another good reason for avoiding this kind of pitched battle if you can.

Population Policy and the Courts

On January 22, 1973, seven Justices of the Supreme Court of the United States (including three Nixon appointees) abruptly eliminated most abortion law restrictions in fifty states and the District of Columbia.

The abortion example is pertinent as a striking illustration of what the courts can do with some pronatalist laws. Courts obviously cannot remake the entire legal/social system; however, many pronatalist laws and practices *can* be eliminated through carefully planned lawsuits (litigation). Such lawsuits, moreover, can be stirred up and helped along by people without legal training. The purpose of this section is to outline what the population-conscious activist can do to identify and resolve those population problems which can be adjudicated by courts.

Courts do not reach out, like legislators, to bring before themselves lawsuits involving a particular subject of current interest. People make lawsuits and other people (judges) rule on those controversies. The task of putting the cast together always rests with members of the public adversely affected by a restrictive law, regulation or clinic custom, and under our legal system it's essential that people and organizations with legitimate complaints about a law be those challenging the law. So if you're an intermediary, acting in someone else's behalf, play down the fact.

Since 1965, when the U.S. Supreme Court invalidated the Connecticut law against *use* of contraceptives, courts have responded more favorably to the notion that the U.S. Constitution protects the individual's access to the means of controlling his reproduction. This right of privacy, implied by the Ninth and/or Fourteenth Amendments to the Constitution, has been recognized by the Supreme Court in the following decisions: *Roe* v. *Wade* (1973); *Eisenstadt v. Baird* (1972); and *Griswold v. Connecticut* (1965). Another important case, which substantially legalized abortion in the District of Columbia, is *United States v. Vuitch* (1971).

Any activist—attorney or otherwise—who tries to reform population policy through court action *must* read and understand those four important U.S. Supreme Court decisions; they are the framework within which judicial decision makers operate in the area of population policy. All proof and argument must be directed toward showing that these cases and their principles apply to the next case, which is the one you stirred up. All law school and political science libraries, libraries in state and federal courthouses, and libraries of bar associations and of many law firms have those decisions, and a helpful librarian will assist you in locating them.

Anatomy of a Population Lawsuit

People who sue, or bring lawsuits, are known as plaintiffs or petitioners. They are the first ingredient of a lawsuit, and when you use litigation as a tool for promoting sane population policy, you should choose individuals or organizations who are seriously affected by the law, regulation or practice under attack. A recent federal case involving Florida's abortion laws and regulations (Poe v. Gerstein) is a good illustration. It involved the parental and spouse consent laws, a regulation against advertising by clinics, and a system of licensing standards for all clinics which was being used to prevent free standing abortion facilities in the state.

ZPG activists, the clergy counseling service and others agreed that the above laws should be attacked, and that a Constitutional basis existed for such an attack. As plaintiff, the counseling service found a recurring flow of pregnant women who were unable or unwilling to obtain parental or spouse consent for abortions. In addition, the director of counseling was a plaintiff who could claim that the laws in question burdened her ability to place prospective patients. These are the kinds of people who are proper plaintiffs from a technical legal standpoint, although an organization such as ZPG or Planned Parenthood may sue, provided it can allege that its members or activities are adversely affected by the law or practice in question.

People and organizations who are sued are called defendants. In the Florida case, all state officials with responsibility for enforcing the challenged abortion law provisions were sued.

When you or your group decide to take an issue to the courts, your lawyer must first file a carefully drawn complaint, along with sev-

---

A Litigation Checklist

Here is an example of the sort of litigation that can bring about a change in population-related laws and practices. This checklist outlines an approach for changing parental consent laws and guidelines through the courts.

☐ *Issue*: Elimination of state and local laws, administrative regulations and guidelines, and hospital or medical facility rules which require consent of parents before minors may receive contraceptives or abortions.

☐ *Plaintiffs Needed*: A physician or professional counselor organization to claim that the parental veto law or rule interferes with his practice and treatment of minors who come to him. An anonymous minor who desires advice or treatment also may sue.

☐ *Defendants to Be Sued*: The State Attorney General or District Attorney in charge of enforcing state or local parental consent law. Also, heads of administrative agencies and hospitals which apply parental consent regulation. Where numerous hospitals impose such a rule, defendants should be sued as a class.

☐ *Mode of Proceeding*: Appropriate plaintiffs file the lawsuit against suitable defendants in the state or federal court most likely to proceed expeditiously toward a result.

☐ *Essential Evidence*: Proof of the law or rule. Proof that the plaintiffs are actually affected, *i.e.*, the organization, counselor or physician is deterred from advising or prescribing, and/or the minor is unable to obtain desired services. Proof of harmful effects of the rule, *i.e.*, the extent of teenage illegitimate pregnancies.

☐ *Arguments*: A comprehensive analysis of the pros and cons of parental consent laws, buttressed by reference to portions of court decisions which emphasize the individual right to privacy. See, in particular, *Eisenstadt* v. *Baird*, *supra*, *Roe* v. *Wade*, *supra*, and *Doe* v. *Bolton*, *supra*.

---

eral other legal documents (including a summons to the defendant or defendants) which set out the facts and legal theory, and request the court to take action against named defendants, or a class of defendants.

After an initial summary, more detailed sections of the complaint are prepared. These describe jurisdiction (how the court has power over the case), the parties (who the plaintiffs are), class action allegations (the nature and size of the public segment affected by the law and represented in the lawsuit), statutory or other provisions in the issue (the statutes, laws, customs, practices, or regulations being contested in the lawsuit, taken verbatim from their sources), facts (details concerning the plaintiff's contention that the impact of the challenged provision is unjustifiable or unduly restrictive), and claims for relief (a recitation of the ways in which the provision is unconstitutional).

After the complaint is filed, your attorneys must assemble evidence and legal arguments. These should be prepared far in advance, to keep the defendants on the defensive. Evidence includes sworn statements as to the accuracy of the allegations made in the complaint.

Your courtroom strategy will vary to meet the needs of the issue you're pursuing. Among the issues which have been successfully dealt with through the courts in state or local cases are: elimination of laws, regulations and guidelines which require spouse consent before a married person may receive an abortion, sterilization or contraceptive care; elimination of regulations which restrict payment of public benefits (Medicaid, state welfare, insurance, maternal health benefits) for contraception, abortion and sterilization; legalization of public advertising of contraceptive services, abortion and sterilization in all media, and gaining access to such media; and elimination of laws, rules and practices whereby hospital governing boards or officers may prohibit provision of contraceptives, abortion and sterilization within the institution, without regard to the needs of physicians and patients. This issue is especialy important in private hospitals which receive federal and/or state funding.

Technical Resources for Bringing Population Litigation

Attorneys, cooperative plaintiffs, legal and medical expertise, and related resources are necessary for bringing lawsuits. No set formula can solve this problem for every city or town, but some generalities are useful.

The Population Law Center in San Francisco has a limited staff, but has handled more lawsuits of this nature than all other groups put together. The address is 230 Twin Peaks Boulevard, San Francisco, California 94114; telephone: (415) 661-2967. Telephone inquiries are likely to bring prompt response in information and materials, but legal help is limited at present. The Center is compiling a national list of "population lawyers" in most large cities which should be particularly useful and will be increased with time.

Local ZPG chapters often have interested affiliated attorneys willing to accept a lawsuit or two at no fee.

The ACLU (American Civil Liberties Union), also with many chapters throughout the United States, has sponsored much litigation concerning abortion, contraception and sterilization.

The NAACP, to date, has not entered this field, but has numerous affiliated attorneys. Often a showing can be made that restrictive laws and practices in this area bear most heavily upon poor and minority groups, and therefore warrant NAACP support and legal representation.

The ASA (Association for the Study of Abortion) in New York City disseminates copies of important medical, legal and social science materials, such as the U.S. Supreme Court opinions in the abortion cases of January, 1973. These provide excellent background material for use in lawsuits, and a publication list can be obtained by writing ASA, 120 West 57th Street, New York, New York 10019, or by calling (212) CI5-2360.

In addition, there are often local law professors, activist attorneys, Legal Services Projects, Legal Aid Societies and related organizations which can be exceedingly helpful with the initiation of lawsuits. Population law questions are fascinating to many attorneys, and the public importance of these problems justifies great effort in seeking out technical assistance. After all, the next Supreme Court decision with profound national implications may be one you stirred up yourself.

The Use of Elections

Elections are the ultimate sanction of the policy game; if you can win in that forum, eventually you will come through everywhere else. Elections, however, are tricky places to try your strength, because issues become confused with personalities and party habits. One way to minimize these "extraneous" factors is to concentrate your efforts in primary races, in which party affiliations are not an issue, and where it's much easier to force a contest on a selected issue. (Of course, the corollary is that your opponents also have the option of picking certain primaries as up-and-down contests to challenge issues on which *you* have been winning in the legislature and the courts.)

To be effective in an election, begin early. Three months is the absolute minimum for preparation of a significant election project, and nine months is probably more realistic. Candidates traditionally believe that $1 of help in May is worth $5 in October. Because campaign work is regulated by both state and federal law (loosely), you probably will need to form some entity through which to co-ordinate your fund-rasing efforts. This entity may have a title as meaningless as the "Good Government Association of Lynn" or as spe-

cific as "Citizens Concerned for Population." It may be formed by you alone for one fight, or in coordination with a combination of your allies for the long run. It must comply with the requirements of election fund laws. A campaign committee can give your efforts focus and visibility; and it can utilize the energies of activists in other groups which do not engage in campaign activities, thus building your support base.

Your population campaign committee can also be effective in the following ways: pressuring candidates to speak out on population issues; evaluating candidates on the basis of their population records, and publicizing these evaluations; endorsing candidates with good positions on your issues, and opposing those with bad ones; briefing candidates on population issues, acquainting them with local facets of population issues, assisting them in writing speeches and statements on population issues; assisting the campaign organizations of good candidates, or those who have special influence and are worth winning over, or who have a good chance to beat particularly bad candidates.

In conducting any of these activities, set yourself a timetable to insure that necessary tasks are begun well ahead of time.

Raising the population issues in a campaign

Organize a letter-writing campaign to daily and weekly newspapers, stressing the population issue. Compare the population positions of various candidates. Keep your letters short and succinct.

Arrange a meeting with an editor or environmental writer of a local paper or a radio/television station. Bring some prominent leaders in the environmental or population movement with you, if you can. Ask the paper or station to consider the positions taken by a candidate on environmental issues in deciding which candidate to endorse. Remind the editor that a population position is an important part of a candidate's environmental record. Offer to provide the station or paper with a summary of the candidate's position, and a copy of the report of the Commission on Population Growth and the American Future (or its state equivalent).

Go to speeches and rallies armed with large catchy posters, literature and buttons, and a list of population-related questions to ask the candidate. Have your supporters dispersed throughout the crowd, so that you are not an obvious group.

Use the same list of questions to call in to radio and TV talk shows featuring candidates. Phone in comments on population positions if a local station features a discussion of the candidates. Have several people try to get through, as the lines are usually very busy.

Arrange to obtain copies of press releases from the campaign. Watch these for good or bad remarks about population-related issues, and have your supporters flood the candidate's office, his opponent and the media with praise for or rebuttal to such remarks.

Rating the candidates

An increasingly effective device in election campaigns is the rating sheet. You must determine in advance which issues are to be included, and whether or not the rating sheet will be based solely on the voting record, on answers to a questionnaire, or on some combination of these and other factors.

A questionnaire has two purposes: first, to evaluate a candidate's position on population issues of your choice, and second, to introduce candidates to your views of what constitutes a population issue. In sending candidates your cover letter, be sure to explain who you are, and why you are sending the questionnaire. Enclose a stamped and addressed envelope.

Population groups which have done this find that only 20 to 40 percent of the candidates will actually reply. You can beef up this rate of return with phone calls to non-repliers. Using this technique, the Miami Chapter of ZPG got an 80 percent response rate.

Endorsements

A questionnaire alone is probably an inadequate basis for endorsing a candidate. Certainly the voting records of known incumbents, and public statements on issues, should be considered before issuing an endorsement. Be certain that any public announcement of support for a candidate or his population stand is acceptable to him. It will certainly alienate a potential friend to come out with a splashy announcement of support if, in his judgment, this costs him votes.

You may print up a sample ballot, indicat-

If you're thinking of working in a political campaign, direct your energies in the following directions. It works.

☐ phone or foot canvassing

☐ arranging teas or coffees for discussion of population issues

☐ fund-raising

☐ running a neighborhood headquarters

☐ assisting with mailing, literature distribution, list preparation, general scout work

☐ showing up at rallies and providing supporters at talk shows

☐ election day activities:
phone bank
distributing sample ballots or palm cards
providing car pools and babysitting for identified supporters
calling voters who have not yet appeared but are favorable
babysitting service for other campaign workers
poll watching

ing voting records of various candidates and those who have been endorsed or opposed. These ballots can be taken into the polling booth by voters. Particularly for many lower-level local races, where most voters feel they are uninformed, the ballot can be influential in swaying votes.

Briefings

It will be useful to prepare a briefing book providing facts that are useful in writing speeches, clippings outlining the local appeal of certain issues, and summaries of what the opponent is saying.

Working for a candidate

Actual manpower and financial resources should be reserved for races where there is a good candidate, where neither victory nor defeat is already assured, and where your efforts are welcome. Like all rules, these are flexible. Sometimes it is worthwhile to work behind a loser as a form of public education, but usually you'll get more accomplished if

your man wins.

Before you meet with a candidate's staff or offer your help, make a careful survey of your resources, how many people you can provide, and how many hours, for what kind of work, each person is willing to pledge. But remember that it is the campaign staff's and your major interest to see that the candidate knows about whatever acts and scenes you put on.

Playing David and Goliath is risky, and you are likely to lose the first time around. Exhaust your possibilities first in other game strategies—Faithful Ally, Mandarin Elite, or People's Will—before you tackle this one.

Of course, the particular strategy you have in mind will depend on your objective. It also will depend on who, when, and where you are, and what resources you have. You should probably start with the simplest game plan that will achieve your goal.

Remember that playing an effective policy

game does not always require a cast of thousands of color-coordinated, uniformed players with unlimited resources. Nor does the measure of your success as a policy player depend on changing the world. Big successes are nice but little ones are also important, and easier to achieve.

If, with the help of the strategies and resources included here, you do achieve one of those little successes, you reform the status quo. You have also become a conscious policy maker.

And we have achieved our goals.

Part Two:
Education

Chapter Nine: Elements of Education

Education can help us all to evaluate, to explore alternatives and, above all else, to make intelligent decisions and act on them. Strangely enough, some very important decisions—between two people, in the community, on campus, at the national level—often are made (or avoided) unconsciously, with surprisingly little reference to reality. These include decisions about contraception, offering services to minors, sex education in schools, land use planning, and zoning. These issues are important—too important to be decided by default. And this is where you come in.

Some people still tend to think of education as a classroom function executed by someone called a teacher, with textbooks and examinations. We must realize that education is not shaped only by the school, but also by the family, business, churches, government, and especially friends. Each time you identify some alternatives or discuss issues with friends or a professor or a class of students, you are acting as an educator. Our purpose in this section of the book is to help you upgrade the decision-making processes we use, individually and collectively, in dealing with population issues. This section will outline three things: possible strategies for programs, targets and elements in education you may wish to develop, and an idea of where you can find and maximize resources.

Education versus Policy

There is a shifting, subtle but significant distinction between education and policy. Both are essential in confronting population issues; both obviously overlap. However, promising education while working for policy change can backfire badly at times. Therefore, it is wise to keep the distinction between them in mind.

Policy actions aim toward influencing someone in a specific direction—usually a direction you have already selected. Education, on the other hand, consists of developing high-quality decisions, testing and exploring alternatives in the presence of thorough information. The educator tries to balance alternatives in a value-fair, not value-loaded, way. Knowing the difference between "fair" and "loaded" in an area as potentially sensitive as population can save a whole program.

Elements of Education

One indication of your success as an educator will be the extent to which personal and group decision making becomes a conscious function of accurate information, rather than of emotion or hidden assumptions. Education implies increasing sophistication. Magical, one-shot solutions are not the goal.

Instructive in this regard are some of the displays and posters that had wide usage in the late 1960's. We saw picture after picture of starving children or, for variation, pictures of white Americans eating dinner with captions like "while you ate dinner tonight, 461 Asians died of starvation." This can be very effective consciousness-raising; however, when they are used in isolation without reference to more information, these displays lead your audience to simple-minded "solu-

Population and Education

If you are thinking of setting up a population education program, or if you merely want to get a clearer, more exact idea of the areas in which such a program might be effective, consider the following issues:

☐ If population refers to more than fertility control, what does "population" mean? Identify specific issues in relation to the individual, the community, the nation.

☐ Individual and Society
–What social structures and stresses affect family size? Employment opportunities? The changing roles of women?
–Are family patterns changing, and if so, what is the effect of these changes on growing elderly populations and alternative family styles?

☐ Family Planning
–What is the role of family planning in population programs? Is it effective in limiting population growth? Should family planning encourage people to have only the number of children they want—no matter how large that number is?
–What forms of family planning services have priority in your community or school? Contraception? Abortion? Sterilization services?

☐ Migration and Distribution
What factors determine where people live? Are these variables consciously planned for optimum population distribution? What *is* "optimum population distribution"?

☐ Population Size
Do international economic and political structures affect population size? Can these structures be manipulated? How and by whom?

☐ Population Stabilization
What is the potential impact of zero population growth on national and local economies? Does a no-growth population mean that we must adapt to a no-growth economy?

☐ Sex Education and Population Education
–What are the components of a good and successful sex education program? What realistic objectives should be set for these programs?
–What is the difference between population education and sex education? What is the purpose of population education?

☐ Population and Environment
How does population growth—as opposed to population distribution—affect our environmental quality?

tions" or into feelings of apathy or futility. In other words, if your work has fostered the "just-sterilize-them-all-in-those-poor-countries" attitude, you have not been involved in education.

An important rule of education is that it should be exciting. The storing of information in memory banks is not. Present the controversial issues and alternatives in an honest way, stimulating interest, not increasing apathy and fatalism. Go beyond simple de-

scriptions of the population crisis or demographic explanations of increasing population size. Involve people—simulations, community surveys and self-tax campaigns are good for this. You should make it obvious that your friends, audience or class have a personal stake, a self-interest, in pursuing a particular topic. This means getting away from a steady diet of abstractions. Specific community issues, identification of personal forces in our lives and their counterparts in other cultures, can be concrete, interesting topics.

One general approach to your education strategy is to show how population issues are related to almost every facet of our lives— where we live, the size of our families, the zoning in our communities. Population issues are intricately woven into our whole life fabric—the thread does not stand alone. Distribution of population and growth affect educational levels, economics, health levels, urban problems, resources, etc. Population is also affected by each of these factors. Dealing with the issues in an integrated context is the most effective approach to good education, and will probably stimulate your audience to action.

Chapter Ten: The Strategies of Exploration and Provocation

The things you find useful in the following pages will depend on who, where and when you are. Take what you find most suitable to your particular situation. Since identifying a problem or issue is a first step in anything, our first strategy involves exploration of the community.

Exploration: Finding Out What Exists

Answers exist only because someone asks questions. In your community, the appropriate question may not be "What is the rate of population growth in Burma?" but rather, "What are the real population-related issues in this community?" Find out what is happening at home. If you spend all your energy decrying high world population and growth rates, your audience will probably remind you that the U.S. population growth appears to be leveling off (although we are adding just under two million people to the population per year). When your concern extends to such topics as investigating the distribution of population, urban migration, death trends—not to mention zoning, housing, opportunities for women—you're on the right track. This may require some community exploration.

Explore and identify your audience as well. People on your campus or in your community may not feel the way you do about population issues. They may not feel anything at all. Don't assume your agenda will be theirs.

One very fruitful, interesting and informal way to gauge what people are thinking is to conduct a survey, as two students at the University of North Carolina did in Chapel Hill, North Carolina. Their objective was to assess attitudes in a cross-section of the town population toward birth control and world population issues. Because they were trying to elicit opinions, not information, they asked simple, open-ended questions, such as "What do you think about family planning or birth control?" and "Is there a world population problem? If so, what is it?"

In two days, interviewing the man on the street with portable tape recorders, they polled eighty-three people. Almost all respondents talked about family planning in terms of economics first, and then as a racial issue. With surprising consistency the whites said that blacks should use more birth control measures. About half of the black respondents said that family planning is being used as an attempt to slow the growth of the black population. The majority of the respondents said that the U.S. has only a slight population problem compared to poorer parts of the world (India was usually cited here). The tapes were so good that they were shortened, spliced and used with great success as discussion-starters in high school classes.

Informal surveys are easy to conduct. If you are a student, people may be more candid with you. Questions should be uniform and simple. Interviews conducted on the street or at work usually provide more open responses than door-to-door interviews. Many people, particularly younger ones, respond more freely to tape recorders than to paper and pencil. If you want to assess the quality of factual knowledge about the population

☐ What kind of sex, population, and environmental education opportunities are available to youth and adults in the community? What prevents more focus on these issues in local schools?

☐ What local and state policies restrict the distribution of birth control information and services? What are eligibility requirements (parenthood, marriage, age limits, parental consent)? Are these based in law or just common practice?

☐ What kind of family planning and fertility-related services are provided (or not provided) in your local community (contraception, pre-birth care, delivery and post-delivery services, child health care, voluntary sterilization, abortion, medical treatment of infertility)?

☐ Does the city or county planning board seem to be planning rational, ordered growth, taking into account economic, environmental, and other aspects of the growth process? Does new housing cost the community more than it brings in with additional tax revenues? Does the planning board operate with an optimum population in mind? The answers to a lot of these questions can be found in these census publications:

—*General Population Characteristics* (PC (1)-B). (One per state)

—*General Social and Economic Characteristics* (PC (1)-C). (One per state)

—*Census Data for Community Action*. U.S. Department of Commerce, Bureau of the Census, Government Printing Office, Washington, D.C. 20409.

The public libraries, city planning office, mayor's office and chamber of commerce often have such census reports on hand. Department of Commerce field offices in forty-two cities also stock these reports for their surrounding areas.

situation in your community, you might ask: Is the U.S. population increasing in size? What are the major changes in our population in the last twenty years? Where do most Americans live? How does immigration affect our present population growth? About what fraction of the people in the U.S. are under the age of twenty-one? Over sixty-five? Is this changing? If so, how?

Community Profiles

Census material can provide important clues to local mysteries. For example, *The Census Data for Community Action*, published by the Bureau of Census, gives an example of ways in which census data could be used in setting up a day-care center:

"Community-supported day-care facilities are often needed in neighborhoods having many working women with small children, or families with no father in the household. The income level of the neighborhood has bearing too, since families with higher incomes can more easily afford adequate private care. Several kinds of useful information about neighborhoods can be found in census reports, such as the number of working mothers who live with their husbands and have children under six years old, the number of families with incomes below the poverty level without a father present, and the average number of children under six years old in such families. This kind of information can help in estimating how many mothers might be involved, and where the best location would be."

In identifying important population trends, it would be useful to develop a profile of the community for the last twenty years or so—

Provocative Population Readings

Good sources for discussion topics—and good subjects of discussion in themselves—are the following books:

Callahan, Daniel, ed. Institute of Society, Ethics and the Life Sciences. "Ethics, Population, and the American Tradition." *Aspects of Population Growth Policy*. Report of the Commission on Population Growth and the American Future: Volume 6, GPO, Washington, D.C. 20402.

Keller, Suzanne. "The Future Status of Women in America." *Demographic and Social Aspects of Population Growth*. Report of the Commission on Population Growth and the American Future: Volume 1, GPO, Washington, D.C. 20402.

Polgar, Steven. "The Possible and the Desirable: Population and Environmental Problems" available from the Department of Anthropology, University of North Carolina, Chapel Hill, N.C. 27514.

Population Reference Bureau, Inc. "Abortion: the Continuing Controversy." *Population Bulletin*, August 1972. Washington, D.C. 20036.

Pradervand, Pierre. "Population and the Third World." *Recycle This Book*, Allan and Hanson (ed.), Wadsworth Publishing Co., Inc., Belmont, Calif. 94002.

Ridley, Jeanne Clare. "On the Consequences of Demographic Change for the Roles and Status of Women." *Demographic and Social Aspects of Population Growth*. Report of the Commission on Population Growth and the American Future: Volume 1, GPO, Washington, D.C. 20402.

Willie, Charles V. "Perspectives from the Black Community." *PRB Selection No. 37*, Population Reference Bureau, Inc., Washington, D.C. 20036.

Wogaman, Philip, ed. *The Population Crisis and Moral Responsibility*. Public Affairs Press, 1973. Washington, D.C.

a feat which is not as difficult as it sounds. Base your profile on census resources, and you'll find you can pinpoint substantive community issues useful not only to you but to local organizations—schools, churches, chambers of commerce, and so on.

Provoke People

Now that you have done some exploration and identified basic population-related issues, you are ready to examine program possibilities. You may already be working with a group that cares enough about an issue—and knows enough about it—to want to do something; but if you don't have those convenient

allies, if your audience or class hasn't really thought about the issue or really doesn't give a damn, you must kindle their interest and help them attend to all aspects of the issue. You can, of course, present your views and leave it at that, but helping your audience think through an issue, rather than merely presenting your own conclusions, is a more interesting and more effective strategy.

Well-planned controversy—the discussion of opposing ideas—is one educational stratagem for group involvement. Educational processes do not necessarily aim to minimize controversy, nor to be one-sided.

The form you choose may be practically

anything—seminar, symposium, rap session, teach-in. One crucial ingredient in stimulating productive controversy is to guarantee group participation. Debates, workshops and dialogues are helpful.

The ideas presented should be germane to the audience. Issues should touch their lives—but be wary of tuning them out. For example, the need for contraceptive services for minors might not stimulate a productive exchange of viewpoints at an open PTA meeting.

Strive for diversity of opinion in the audience. Try to fill many points on the continuum of opinion with special invitations to key students, community leaders and politicians.

The issue publicized should be a controversial one. Something dealing with these population-related topics would be provocative: black genocide, third world development, women's roles and rights, abortion, local population distribution policies, the ethics of governmental incentive programs and family planning.

New Bill of Rights

One theme which might provoke your audience more than you bargained for is a discussion of a new Bill of Rights. Caroline Bird, author of *Born Female* and *The Crowding Syndrome*, has suggested that some rights we have always regarded as absolute and natural will have to go.

One such right is the absolute right to life. Many observers now believe that the unrestricted right to bear children may expose the planet to intolerable risks of overpopulation.

Should population-control measures be coercive? Dubious also, in this view, is the right to live as long as medical technology can keep you breathing. Exorbitantly expensive methods of prolonging life now exist, but they cannot be offered to all. We may have to ration our medical technology.

Another disputable right is the right to consume as much as you can buy. It is obvious that you no longer have the right to burn soft coal in New York City, water your lawn in a drought, buy all the gasoline you want, or kill ostriches to wear their feathers in your hats, but we may soon have to ration such intrinsically limited commodities as apartment space in Manhattan.

Then what about the right to build your house to your pleasure? The more people there are, the more rules there must be to insure that one house does not obstruct the view or otherwise interfere with its neighbors. There will also have to be laws protecting natural resources and wildlife.

This brings into dispute the right to ownership. There will be a growing list of products prohibited to private ownership. The private production of commercial goods and services will inevitably be restricted by the expansion of publicly-controlled activities. The right to privacy itself becomes dubious when population density reaches the saturation point.

And finally, we may have to change our minds about the right of access to all public places. Museums, the galleries of Congress, hospital waiting-rooms and courtrooms cannot accommodate all the people who may

wish to exercise their "right" to visit them, and safety may require that this right be rationed. In the future, the terms of access to various places will have to be defined and articulated more explicitly than at present. All of these points should allow for a very lively exchange of viewpoints.

Another program possibility—although perhaps not so involving because it is not so provocative—is a review of new major reports on population, such as the article entitled "A Blueprint for Survival" in *The Ecologist*, a new British journal concerned with environmental problems. This report calls for eventual reduction of the population of the United Kingdom to 30 million, well below the present figure of 56 million. The twenty-two-page article, along with twenty pages of appendices, can be found in *The Ecologist* 2 (January 1972), pp. 1-22, 24-43. (To order *The Ecologist*, write to 73 Molesworth Street, Wadbridge, Cornwall, England.) A second report, *The Limits to Growth* (New York: Universe Books, 1972), was released in March, 1972. It deals with problems of growth in a variety of areas, including population, technology and resources, as well as the present and future state of global equilibrium. In some circles, *The Limits to Growth* has become extremely controversial, and for this reason, as well as for its basic message, it is important reading.

Required reading for anyone concerned with population is *Population and the American Future*, the report of the Commission on Population Growth and the American Future.

The principal thrust of the report, which was released in March, 1972, is that none of our problems will be easier to solve with continued population growth; yet the report also attempts to make recommendations for government policy. It has already been the center of wide public reaction and controversy which will continue over the next several years. A copy may be obtained from the U.S. Government Printing Office or as a Signet Book (New York: New American Library, 1972) on newsstands as a $1.50 paperback.

Chapter Eleven: Create, Using the Media

There are many different media for you to use when dealing with population issues: video tapes, audio-visual material, exhibits, books, movies, press services. With a bit of care these resources can be used to stimulate and inform rather than lecture to and bore your audience.

Videotapes

"We forget that the antitheses of anger, polarization, ugliness and war are things that we create actively." This reminder comes from Martha Stuart, a communicator who created a Chicago television series called *Are You Listening*. She believes that what is wrong with education today is also wrong with educational television—but the latter is capable of tuning out larger numbers than any college or university. Both tend to say: "You are out of it, so learn this material."

If you have access to videotape equipment on your campus, you can try your hand at what communications theorists call "affective television," a medium that poses questions about which the audience thinks and decides; it does not get people or groups into stereotypes; it lets people speak for themselves.

From a thirty-second spot to a thirty-minute discussion, you may be able to capture this technique simply by letting two people or more (not over twelve) "be themselves" in open exchange about an issue which is important to them. As an alternative, survey people individually and splice their opinions together. Whichever form you choose, the issues should be real to the individuals involved. In other words, topics such as economic development or contraceptive research probably won't make it. Rather, choose the concerns you and your friends feel strongly about—birth control and services on your campuses or where you work, abortion traumas, condom machines in dormitories, day care facilities, land-use planning.

The materials you construct may be used effectively in several settings: as discussion-starters for a classroom; as a documentary of opinion for community groups; or as TV and radio spots.

ARTHUR RICKERBY/TIME-LIFE PICTURE AGENCY

Flicks

Forget most population films done before 1970—for the most part they are doom, gloom and oversimplification.

But don't dismiss the medium! Recently some rather good film and filmstrip materials have surfaced. Each of the following films could be the major part of a program on population, or you could order them all as parts of a multi-media week on population issues. You have tremendous diversity in both content and style among these seven offerings.

1) *Population and the American Future* is the film version of the Report of the Commission on Population Growth and the American Future; and you can get it for the asking. If you saw it over PBS television in November, 1972, you know its potential for provoking discussion. The Commissioners themselves had final editorial say, so the issues are treated fairly. For easier program or classroom use, the sixty-minute TV version is divided into two thirty-minute segments and is accompanied by a guide for discussion and action. You can purchase it from the Fisher Film Group, 216 East 49th Street, New York, New York 10017, for $300, or get it on free loan from Modern Talking Pictures, 2323 Hyde Park Road, New Hyde Park, New York 11040. But order it early. It takes two months to get it.

2) *Issues in Population*: *Where the Experts Disagree* is a twenty-eight-minute slide or filmstrip and sound program presenting a much-needed balanced approach to

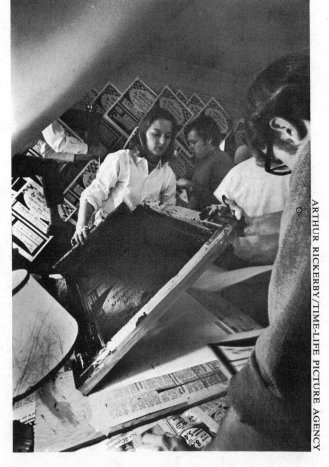

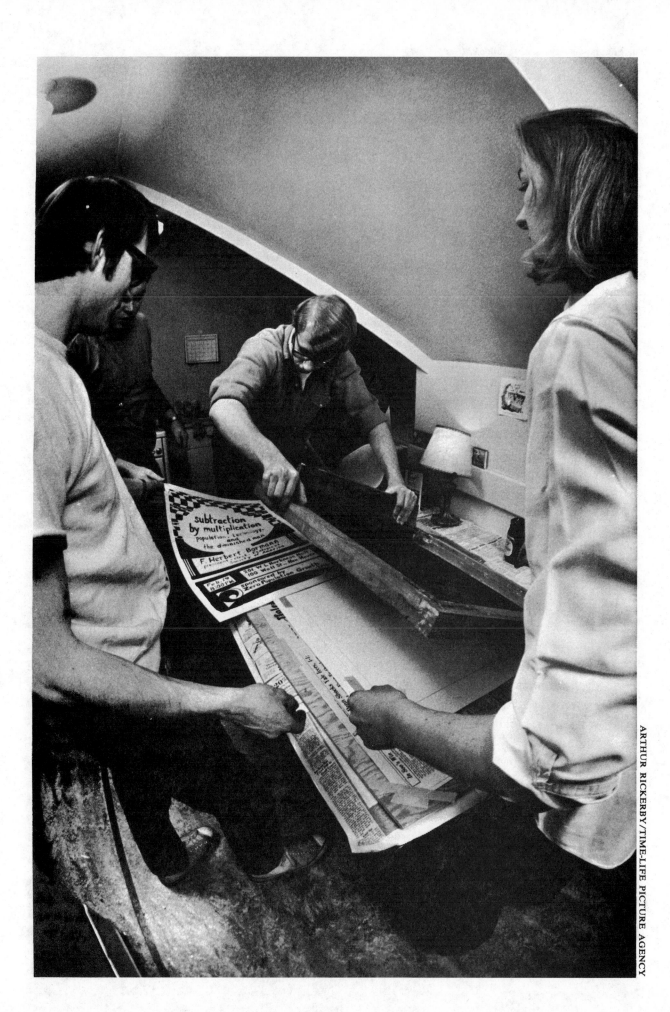

population problems. After a brief discussion of world population growth, several issues are raised, with differing viewpoints given by experts such as Bernard Berelson, Paul Ehrlich and Norman Ryder. Among the topics covered are: population and food, population and the environment, and population growth and policies in the U.S. The program tries to give equal time to various viewpoints. Both the slide show ($45) and the filmstrip ($20) come with a viewer's guide and are available from Audio-Visuals Productions, International Population Program, Social Science Building, Cornell University, Ithaca, New York 14850.

Films from the Census Bureau:

— *We* is a color film produced in thirty- and fifteen-minute versions by the U.S. Bureau of the Census. It presents the key findings of the 1970 Census—the growth movement and characteristics of the U.S. population. For high school audiences.

— *Fact Finder for the Nation* tells the story of the Bureau of the Census in thirty- and fifteen-minute color film versions.

Both films are available free of charge from National Audio-visual Center, Washington, D.C. 20409.

4) *A Single Step*, produced by the College Program of Planned Parenthood-World Population, centers on student concern and action in the areas of ecology, population limitation and birth control on campus.

This twenty-eight-minute color program can be rented for $12.50 from Planned Parenthood—World Population, 810 Seventh Avenue, New York, New York 10019.

5) *About Sex* is a film concerning the human and practical aspects of sexuality. Hariette Surovell, one of the high-school student founders of the Coalition for Relevant Sex Education, says "All in all, I would call *About Sex* 'about perfect.' It is exactly what we've been waiting for." Recently this two-part film won a New York film festival award.

This twenty-three-minute color film is available for $25 rental from Texture Films, Inc., 1600 Broadway, New York, New York 10019 (with study guide upon request).

6) *Tragedy of the Commons* is a controversial film, and should be used as such. The film, which follows a population analogy of an overgrazed pastureland, is visually exciting. Some complain that in expressing the gravity of the population crisis, it oversimplifies a complex issue and moralizes too much.

You can make effective use of *Tragedy of the Commons* with the discussion guide. It is available for $35 rental from King Screen Productions, 320 Aurora Avenue North, Seattle, Washington 98109.

7) *Population, Boom or Doom?* This film is a study of four issues from the Report of the Commission on Population Growth and the American Future: population numbers, current and projected; sex ed-

ucation; contraception and abortion; and immigration. It emphasizes the quality of life rather than the population crisis.

It is a sixty-minute, 16mm color film (1973). ABC Media Concepts, 1330 Avenue of the Americas, New York, New York 10019. Purchase price, $250; rental $25. (Grades 9–adult)

Adapt It

Make a near-success your complete success. There are a few audio-visual efforts which just don't quite make it in terms of potential media appeal, but you could use one of these near-successes and adapt it to the needs, likes and dislikes of your community or campus.

This may mean creating your own audio-visual portion to complete an A-V program. You could, for instance, do a tape to accompany and clarify the slide series from the PRB *Population Bulletins*. Even better, supplement these graphics with other kinds of slides—nature scenes, people pictures—anything which might make the presentation more fun and stimulating. (These slides are available from the Population Reference Bureau, Inc., 1755 Massachusetts Avenue, N.W., Washington, D.C. 20036.) Or you could design a new visual half to the film strip or slide show *Issues in Population*: *Where the Experts Disagree*, produced by Peter Wernick of Cornell's International Population Program. Although the tape portion of this program is already very, very good, the black and white visuals were done on a shoestring budget. They could

be improved to make the entire package more interesting and provocative.

Newspapers

If paper and print were as passé as the McLuhanites would have us believe, newspapers and publishing houses would be out of business. Assuming significant communication is still carried out in print, it is important to select the appropriate method for delivering what you want to say. Under certain conditions, putting out your own leaflet or newspaper may be effective. It is often easier on your man-hours and pocketbook to write for an established readership. Campus journals, community newspapers and regional periodicals can be helpful allies.

A 1970 creation hatched by three college students working for the Institute for the Study of Health and Society in Washington, D.C. was a *Population Pressbook*, in which appeared cartoons, fillers and short articles (300-800 words). These were packaged to "make the job easy" for campus and community editors, who didn't have access to other sources of information. You could try something similar. If you offer such a "package deal," however, you will need to re-contact the editor or writer throughout the year to gently remind him of your gift and to offer more recent and locally relevant stories.

Sources of information for such articles or packages are practically unlimited. Some of the most fruitful are the U.S. Department of Commerce *News*, Washington, D.C. 20230 (have your local paper put on this press re-

lease list); *Family Planning Perspectives*, Planned Parenthood Federation of America, 515 Madison Avenue, New York, New York 10022; *Concerned Demography*, Center for Demography and Ecology, 3224 Social Science Building, University of Wisconsin, Madison, Wisconsin 53706 ($2 per subscription); *Population Bulletin*, Population Reference Bureau, Inc., 1755 Massachusetts, Avenue, N.W., Washington, D.C. 20036 ($5 student subscription, or 50 cents per copy; there are recent Bulletins on China, third world development, abortion, Russia, women's roles); *Population and the American Future*, the Report of the Commission on Population Growth and the American Future, U.S. Government Printing Office, Washington, D.C. 20515 ($1.75).

Books in the Stacks

One important backup step which, in the end, may give you considerable mileage is that of stocking your local (campus or community) libraries. After all, when you get a few people fired up about the tricky population issues, someone has to supply fuel.

If you approach the acquisitions librarian, be prepared to offer some leads on appropriate sources of *current* population literature. Fortunately, the two major indices your librarian uses probably already have added population as a topic. The Public Affairs Information Service now indexes the *Population Bulletin* and the *Population Index*. The Social Science and Humanities Index now lists population and family planning publications.

Two other publications should be called to the librarian's attention. One is *Overview: A Journal of Population Libraries* (1972, Chapel Hill, Carolina Population Center, Chapel Hill, North Carolina 27514—free); another is the *Directory of Population Libraries and Information Centers in the United States*, edited by Bates Buckner and Marilyn McIntyre (Carolina Population Center, Chapel Hill, North Carolina 27514—$7.00).

You might also get to your "roving" librarian. Many rural and urban areas have mobile libraries which move from one neighborhood to another. Why not suggest a small special shelf for population materials?

Chapter Twelve: Turn Around Academia

Like the New York subways at rush hour, public school curricula tend to be overcrowded. And teachers, like subway drivers who follow fixed routes, often prescribe lists of materials and books which must be followed. Yet there are many opportunities—in social science, biological sciences, mathematics, even in English courses—for introducing population concepts.

Changing the curriculum, or only one course, is essentially a problem of changing people. You must be prepared to argue the importance of population education, the concern and the interest young people have for population issues and, most importantly, the legitimate role these issues play in today's curriculum.

Push the Public Schools

Population education deals with the relationships between population change and the individual, community, nation, world. The topics of population education are myriad. For example: rural-urban migration; women's roles; population and poverty; food, nutrition and population change. The extent to which sex education is incorporated into the much broader world-view of population will depend on the emphasis of a population education course. (Is it oriented toward the family? The nation? Migration issues? And so on.) Sex education is often just a rehash of anatomical language, but *population* education has a much broader scope. Sometimes sex education is too controversial to be handled by a school, but population education, while immensely interesting, need not be so controversial. Whether you are working with a public system or an individual teacher, you must decide what is most appropriate to your situation.

You should feel successful if you contact, convince and are able to offer resources to even one teacher. But it's even better if you manage to do the same for a curriculum supervisor, for through this key person, you may indirectly reach ten, twenty, maybe fifty other teachers in the system.

The first and simplest step is to provide some sound but provocative teaching resources: magazines or even planned curriculum programs that deal with population. When passing on, or just recommending, such material, point out that in most cases well-established education organizations have been responsible for putting it together; organizations like the National Council for the Social Studies, the National Education Association, and the Sociological Resources for the Social Studies (which is funded by the National Science Foundation).

It's always better to offer a concrete program or list of resource materials if you want to bring population education into the classroom. The materials listed in the following box are easy to obtain and are basic to an understanding of population issues.

Once you have provoked a genuine commitment from a curriculum supervisor or group of teachers, you should see that the teachers are given some kind of training in population education. Such training can range

□ The April 1972 (special population) issue of *Social Education*, the journal of the National Council for the Social Studies. At least one teacher and/or the school librarian should have this issue tucked away somewhere; copies are also available from N.C.S.S. at 1201 16th Street, N.W., Washington, D.C. 20036, for $1.50.

□ Reprints of "Sources and Resources" (excerpted from the April 1972 issue of *Social Education*), a 32-page annotated bibliography of teaching and student reading materials. Listings of films and organizations are available free from the Population Reference Bureau, Inc., 1755 Massachusetts Avenue, N.W., Washington, D.C. 20036.

□ The National Education Association recently published *Environment and Population: A Sourcebook for Teachers*, which includes a conceptual scheme, discussions, classroom activities and references for junior and senior high courses in Contemporary Issues, Family Life, Health, History, Science and Sociology. Available from NEA Publications, 1201 16th Street, N.W., Washington, D.C. 20036, for $3.75.

□ The Sociological Resources for the Social Studies have produced a fine collection of high school units dealing with population, *Episodes in Social Inquiry* (Allyn and Bacon, 1972). These are eight- to twelve-day units in the form of Student Resources and Instructors' Guides and all are available from the publisher. Of particular interest

are:
Family Size and Society
Migration Within the United States
Population Change: A Case Study of Puerto Rico
Roles of Modern Women

□ *Options for Population and the American Future* is a study guide to *Population and the American Future* (the Report of the Commission on Population Growth and the American Future). The material is designed for use at junior high, senior high and college levels and includes learning objectives, discussions and activity suggestions. Available from Population Reference Bureau, Inc., 1755 Massachusetts Avenue, N.W., Washington, D.C. 20036, for 50 cents handling charge.

□ *Interchange* is a population education newsletter, published bi-monthly by the Population Reference Bureau for secondary level teachers. Each issue contains notice of the latest teaching materials and training opportunities, an activity sketch and a brief description of "what's happening" in the field. Subscription is $2 from P.R.B., 1755 Massachusetts Avenue, N.W., Washington, D.C. 20036.

□ *Intercom* is a publication of the Center for War/Peace Studies which focuses on global problems. Past issues have dealt with population, world development, and the concept of spaceship Earth. Each issue costs $1.50, and is available from the Center for War/Peace Studies, 218 East 18th Street, New York, New York 10003.

from the intensive six-week—or longer—summer institute to the one-hour workshop. In ideal cases, teachers are paid to attend. Often they receive in-service credit toward a salary increase. The present trend seems to be running in favor of teachers doing their in-service work during regular school hours.

Unfortunately, this means that, except for summer workshops, any in-service work will probably have to be designed for short, intensive blocks of time. Don't expect teachers to participate in a training effort which demands time and/or travel unless there is a personal payoff.

As an alternative to lengthy training programs, you might think about short, intensive one- to two-hour sessions held in the school building during the school day. Teachers from the school, or from several neighboring schools, could attend these sessions, go back to their own classrooms and actually try out ideas presented, and then meet again later that day to talk over what had happened. This would make in-service work as directly and immediately useful as possible. It also would help to assure instant feedback and evaluation.

Another possibility is to have your group—or whoever is presenting the workshops—actually teach a class of one or more of the teachers enrolled. The teachers could look on and then discuss the substance and the methods of the lesson. Then the teachers would teach the same lesson to their own classes and

come together later to exchange impressions and evaluations. All this could be done locally, during the school day, which would avoid excessive travel time and assure that the teachers in the workshop were all teaching the same general material. In the past, workshops that included teachers from widely different school settings suffered from a lack of common interests, backgrounds and concerns, but keeping in-service activities localized partially overcomes this difficulty.

Choose the kind of workshop that works best for you, always remembering that both of the workshop models suggested above meet local needs, don't cost much, and provide both a chance for local teachers to exchange ideas and a means by which students can play an integral role in an in-service program.

On the College Campus:
Expect Problems—Play Politics

On any college or university campus there are real barriers to the promotion of population education programs—even when enlightened faculty members get into the act. Departmental and inter-departmental politics are always at work, and professors who are concerned about population need support—particularly from students, when they can't get it from fellow faculty. So your first task is to muster adequate student interest and demand—and provide evidence of it. Offer this evidence—in the form of a petition, a poll or whatever—to a faculty committee, which can then put the machinery in motion to get a new course, or course change, under way.

You may also bump into interdepartmental rivalry, an unfortunate complication, since population is a logical candidate for multidisciplinary study. Some biologists, for instance, believe they have always given adequate attention to human population and feel that sociologists are only inadequate psychologists. Some sociologists, on their side, dismiss demographers as "number crunchers." But you have a role to play in bringing these people together.

Another potential problem, which has more to do with effective teaching than with implementation, is the crisis-orientation many teachers are likely to bring to the study of population. When courses of these instructors attempt to change the values of students rather than to extend their knowledge, population is no longer a discipline. It becomes an intellectually limited field that keeps chasing the latest policy fads.

Students who are critical of courses that stress access to contraception as the solution to population problems, however, say that these courses do no more than consciousness raising—which the media have already accomplished. To students with this perspective, lecturers on family planning are less informative about factors that affect population growth than sociologists who examine population phenomena from a structural and institutional approach. It also seems more convincing on a personal level. Students say contraception will not determine their own family size so much as provide the means to realize it. Career alternatives, access to jobs, the community in which they live after college, and changes in women's and men's roles are more likely to influence their family size. Faculty members may not be aware of this kind of criticism, but you may be in a position to warn them of the need for a more open-ended approach to population study. You could suggest that the scope of course offerings be broadened to address such topics as: population and the law (local, state, national, and international), population distribution and migration, population policy and political power, or population and women's roles.

You may also want to draw your professors' attention to *Teaching Notes on Population: An Occasional Newsletter for College Teachers*, edited by Parker G. Marden. This offers evaluations of textbooks and other teaching materials, as well as ideas for presenting different aspects of population study for undergraduates. It is available free from the Foreign Area Materials Center, 60 East 42nd Street, New York, New York 10017.

Changing the Usual: Population as a Component of College or University Courses

Getting population concepts into *current* courses on your campus is often much easier than starting a separate population course. Population issues can easily be considered in the context of ongoing courses in political science, economics, sociology, education, history and biology. It doesn't take much imagination to see the linkages between various population issues and the basic concepts of each of these discipline areas. But you may want to give your professor a push with outlines, references, and so on. Obviously, the more help you can provide, the less difficult the change will appear.

History

You might think History is one discipline where the connection with population issues may not seem particularly clear, but it certainly can be related to population from at least two points of view. The first takes into account the movements, trends, phenomena and innovations that have had a significant effect on population growth and distribution—examples of which would be the advent of and reliance on the potato in the Old World (Europe, Ireland); historical influence of disease and disease control; social makeup of colonial systems; the emergence of New World crops in Asia; and colonization. Another point of view would consider what demographic trends have affected history and political systems—changes in the age structure of a population, changes in family size, changes in the size and density of a population, differential population growth rates among different social classes and ethnic groups, or migration. Suggest to your professor that he or she ask some or all of the following questions about the political or historical effects of population. How are population changes perceived? To what extent do they have political effects? Do the demographic changes have an independent and direct political consequence? How are demands

upon the political and administrative framework affected by population changes? What are the effects of population changes on the political and social interaction of groups and the distribution of political power within the society?

You could also offer your history professor the following bibliography:

"Historical Population Studies," *Daedalus*, Spring, 1968.

Polgar, Steven, "Population History and Population Policies from an Anthropological Perspective," *Current Anthropology*, April, 1972.

Weiner, Myron, "Political Demography: An Inquiry into the Political Consequences of Population Change," *Rapid Population Growth*. The Johns Hopkins Press, 1971.

Wrigley, E. A., *Population and History*. London: World University Library, 1969.

Engineering and Population

The 1960's and 1970's have presented some grim possibilities to the world: pollution, pesticides, drugs, overpopulation, overloaded cities, loss of privacy and loss of control due to complexity. But most people, except for a few skeptics here and there, tend to regard such problems as essentially solvable by use of better, more efficient technology.

Most of us have taken part in discussions on the question of whether "improved technology is our true savior." Unfortunately, in the minds of many, this matter is not a question but a basic assumption, a *sine qua non*—technology is the universal savior. In what ways are the ethical implications of such scientific breakthroughs suggested in your engineering department's courses?

Environmental engineers are by no means the only engineers who are immediately and practically involved in population issues. Architects and technicians who are involved in waste disposal, or highway construction, or building—all will have an effect on the population problem. How are the applied sciences influencing the growth of communities? Are they part of the planning process? There are numerous problems addressed by architects, chemists and engineers which logically demand simultaneous analysis of population growth and distribution outcomes. Why shouldn't your engineering courses take into account this "technology assessment"—the evaluation of the likely consequences of a technological development? Technology assessment means different things to different people, and so it offers a wide range of study possibilities. For those concerned primarily with environmental quality, technology assessment means the evaluation of technical changes and their impact on various *environmental* goals and resources. For those concerned with the measurement of social change, it means the use of new tools to monitor the impacts of technical changes *on society*. For those concerned with the need for guiding technical change, it means an attempt to project the probable impacts of specific technologies. If your engineering professor wants to consider any of these issues, he might find the following reading list a help:

Banfield, *The Unheavenly City*

Dubos, *So Human an Animal*

Erhlich, *Population, Resources, Environment*

Ferkiss, *Technological Man*

Foreign Policy Association, *Toward the Year 2018*

Forrester, "Counterintuitive Behavior of Social Systems," *Technology Review*, January 1971

Friedman, L., *Government and Slum Housing*

Galbraith, *The New Industrial State*

Hardy, *Mathematician's Apology*

Lewis, A., *Of Men and Machines*

Michael, *The Unprepared Society*

Miller, A., *The Assault on Privacy*

Morrison, *Men, Machines, and Modern Times*

National Academy of Sciences, *Technology: Processes of Assessment and Choice*

Roszak, *The Making of a Counter-Culture: Reflections on the Technocratic Society and Its Youthful Opposition*

Schwartz, *Overskill*

Sennett, *The Uses of Disorder: Personal Identity and City Life*

Taviss, *The Computer Impact*

Toffler, *Future Shock*

Vonnegut, *Player Piano*

If a New Course is in Order . . .

If infusing population concepts into existing courses is difficult, the initiation of a new course is like pulling teeth without novocain —difficult and painful. Yet, it is done all the

If you want to put together a new course on population problems and policies, it is always best to have a concrete outline or proposal to show your professor or department or faculty committee. *Options*, a study guide based on the official report of the Commission on Population Growth and the American Future, is a useful syllabus and you could certainly base a course on it. (It is available from the Population Reference Bureau, Inc., 1755 Massachusetts Avenue NW, Washington, D.C. 20036.) Another possible course outline, also based on the Commission's report, could cover the following points:

I. Introduction: An explanation of history and goals of the Commission report

II. Individuals as population actors—analysis of the interaction between society and the individual in determining population policy

III. Population growth and distribution—implications of population growth for the United States, role of immigration in American society, problems of population distribution

IV. Population and the American future—a proposal for population stabilization, discussion of its effect on quality of life

If your course needs are sociological and international in scope, an excellent course idea would be a review of the differing causes of population growth, followed by an exploration of the consequences for population density and urban-rural settlement, food and natural resources, economic and social development, and political relationships both within and between nations.

By reaching prospective teachers with a course in population education, you ultimately may reach a whole other generation. A syllabus for a course in this area might include the following topics:

I   The history and objectives of population education

II The possible content of population education courses—data, consideration of social values and pressures, present policy

III Knowledge and attitudes of youth on population issues

IV Psychological considerations in population education—influence of developmental, secular and educational changes

V   Educational considerations — relevant and value-fair teaching

VI Implementation of population education—reaching the teacher and the student, using different media of instruction

For a course like this last one, the following references would be useful:

Brown, Jerry L., *A Plan for an Instructional Unit on Population Dynamics*. ERIC/Chess, 855 Broadway, Boulder, Colorado 80302.

Population Bulletin. Population Reference Bureau, Inc., 1755 Massachusetts Avenue, N.W., Washington, D.C. 20036. Spring 1973. $.50

Seltzer, Judith and Horsley, Kathryn, editors, *Proceedings of the National Conference on Population Education*. Population Reference Bureau, Inc., 1755 Massachusetts Avenue, N.W., Washington, D.C. 20036. $1.00

Viederman, Stephen, editor, *Social Education*. National Council for the Social Studies. 1201 16th Street, N.W., Washington, D.C. 20036. April 1972. $1.50

time, and you might as well have some say in the process.

The real work lies in influencing the departmental academic hierarchy. In the process, don't limit your ideas to the traditional course offering. You may want a student-run seminar: a multi-departmental course calling on a number of teachers and/or community members. For instance, why have your WASPish sociology professor deal with the issue of population control as race genocide when there are perfectly healthy black spokesmen right in your community? Why accept a panel of middle-aged males discussing the psychological effects of abortion, when you have sitting in the class young women with experience of its realities?

Part Three: Services

Chapter Thirteen: The Sexual Revolution vs. The Quiet Revolution

Changing policy and educating the public are two ways of dealing with the population problem. Another integral area of endeavor is that of providing contraceptive services and information—clinics, counseling, hotlines, referrals—that are easily accessible to everyone who wants them. One of the best places to start when you're concerned about the availability of these services is on the college or university campus, for the campus is society in miniature—and, more important, it is the society that forms the policy-maker of tomorrow. Yet the kind of preventive medicine that can strike at the heart of the population problem is difficult for the student to obtain.

Consider that in the last five years, the increasing number of students on campus, co-educational dorm living, the greater heterogeneity of the student body, and the seemingly dramatic weakening of traditional restraints and values regarding sex and sex roles—all have altered the nature of the student's experience on the college campus. Furthermore, developments in the larger society—such as the eighteen-year-old vote, the legalization of abortion, and the spread of candid treatment by the mass media of sexual matters—all affect sexuality and social life at the university. One of the most dramatic changes may be the increase in the number of non-virgins on campus during the late 1960's and early 1970's.

In light of these changes, the university today must assume responsibility for constructing as many resources as possible to meet the sexual health, education and counseling needs of the students, with particular attention to those student groups frequently neglected: the graduate students, those who live off-campus, minority or foreign students, married couples and homosexuals. Our college campuses, our young people, all of us, are in the midst of a true sexual revolution, but we are not playing the significant role in it which we might think we are. In fact, we are actually the consenting victims of the revolt. Despite our confidence that we know all there is to know about free relationships between consenting adults in private, the truth is that most of us have had the same formal sex education as our parents—none at all. We have educated ourselves through books and movies, and we have allowed our peers and our parents to educate us, either directly or indirectly. And that's the way it will stay, from now until eternity, unless someone decides to negate the premises of the so-called sexual revolution. Once we have established that we of today have the same wants, needs and desires as our parents had in the past, we can begin a quiet revolution, one of health, education and counseling, that comes to terms with our sexuality. It's already happening; on a number of campuses across the country students have approached the questions of contraception, population and provision of services from a multitude of angles. At Cornell College in Iowa, students organized a week-long symposium on sexuality; the University of Minnesota holds an annual Sex Week. At Yale University, Dr. Philip Sarrel teaches a course, organized by students, dealing with changing

How does a quiet revolution work on campus? Students at the University of North Carolina at Chapel Hill felt their university wasn't helping them with the questions and problems they had on different aspects of their sexual lives. They intended to do more than just discuss their problems among themselves; they were ready to organize. Students began putting their heads together in the summer of 1969. By 1973, students and administration were coordinating one of the finest efforts in the country to meet the needs of those on the college campus.

In those four years, the students have:

☐ Written and distributed on campus a booklet, "Elephants and Butterflies . . . and Contraceptives," describing birth control, abortion and venereal diseases for the students. Today over 55,000 copies of this booklet have been sold to colleges across the country. A question-and-answer column of the same name now appears in college newspapers throughout the southeast.

☐ Coordinated for students—in the dormitories and in their classes—lectures, discussion groups, films and displays about various aspects of sex.

☐ Designed and coordinated "Topics in Human Sexuality," a three-hour credit course consisting of major lectures and small group discussions, meeting one night a week for sixteen weeks. About 280 students enroll in the course, one of the most popular on campus, every semester.

☐ Established the Human Sexuality Information and Counseling Service with thirty trained volunteer students and townspeople. The service, handling about sixty-five cases per week, provides peer counseling, information and referral concerning sexual problems and questions.

☐ Did a random survey of the sexual knowledge, attitudes and behavior prevalent on campus; it is still being used to establish new campus programs and policies.

sexual mores. In addition, he and his wife work as a team in sexual counseling. From the University of Colorado at Boulder to Allegheny College in Meadville, Pennsylvania, students have taken a less traditional educational approach and organized rap sessions in dormitories and sorority and fraternity houses. Students at Berkeley, the University of North Carolina, Buffalo, the University of Houston and other schools have written excellent pamphlets describing contraceptive techniques. Students have opened the doors of change on what is directly affecting them. In the following pages, we describe what was and is taking place on campus in the areas of: birth-control information centers, problem pregnancy, fertility control services, human sexuality counseling, etc.

As each campus is unique, each one's accomplishment indicates a tailor-made approach and solution to an existing situation. These developments can serve as models for other campuses, but only with the understanding that there is no limit to the possibilities, and no one right way.

This and the next chapter will try to examine in detail the issue of human sexuality as it relates to campus life; it will attempt to show how you can come to grips with this issue; and it will name some names, telling you about some other people who are already working to bring about the quiet revolution.

☐ Reached out to other campuses to help them begin such programs.

☐ Designed and co-sponsored the "North Carolina Workshop on Problem Pregnancy Counseling," attended by over 500 counselors representing 93 of the state's 100 counties.

☐ Edited and co-authored *Problem Pregnancy and Abortion Counseling*, the first handbook in the United States written for problem-pregnancy counselors, now sold nationally by Family Life Publications.

The campus administration, in turn, has:

☐ Helped fund and provided space for the "Topics in Human Sexuality" course.

☐ Provided contraceptive prescriptions and counseling, pregnancy counseling and referral, and a special gynecological clinic through the Student Health Service.

☐ Hired a Health Educator to act as liaison between the students and the Health Service as well as to coordinate materials, lectures and discussion groups on topics such as sexuality.

☐ Begun writing a new booklet for the students that covers the many aspects of sexuality, not just information related to sexual intercourse.

☐ Put the professional staff of the Student Health Service to work for the student-run Human Sexuality Information and Counseling Service, both training staff and answering by telephone any questions too difficult for the student counselors to handle.

The University of North Carolina is a good example of how the university community—students, faculty, administration—can work together in planning and implementing programs on sexuality. For more information on their projects, write the Human Sexuality Information and Counseling Service, Box 51, Carolina Union, UNC, Chapel Hill, North Carolina 27514.

All of them are eager to share the insights they have gained in the field.

What is our sexuality?

One thing our sexual revolution forgot to teach us was what *sexuality* really means. *Sexuality* is our need to express ourselves through our bodies. It is a basic part of our maleness or femaleness, our self-image, our identity, our personality, our human awareness and development. Sexuality is a part of our desire for personal satisfaction and happiness, and it stimulates our need to establish fulfilling relationships with others.

Sex is a function of sexuality. Sex is not something we do which is separate from ourselves. It is not a goal, not an objective. It is an integral part of us. We cannot work toward gaining it. Sex does not *establish* who we are, it *expresses* who we are.

If our sexuality is a part of us, what are our responsibilities to it? First, we can get in touch with our own sexuality: our needs, our desires, our pleasures, our fantasies, our functioning. We need to know the goods and the bads of our sexual personality. Unfortunately, we sometimes get wrapped up in faulty logic, thinking that the more we know, the more responsible we have to be; the more responsible we are, the more easily we can be blamed if something goes wrong. The upshot of this is the feeling that if we don't really understand our desires, our needs, our functions, we can feel justified in pleading innocent to charges of sexual misconduct. Few of us realize that if we *do* understand and accept our sexuality, decisions concerning our sexual life are not so frightening.

Our second responsibility to our sexuality can be to accept and be comfortable with sex as a natural and integral part of our lives. It is not enough to accept certain aspects of sex "in theory." Sexuality and sex are real, alive and a part of each of us.

Our third responsibility can be to *express our sexuality* to ourselves and to others, especially to those we love. This requires that we become more open about our feelings than we have been in the past. In this new openness we expose our true selves more, and we can become more vulnerable to others. But if we have fulfilled our first two responsibilities —coming to terms with our sexuality and accepting what we find—then this vulnerability can be rewarding. We can then realize the need we have for sexual expression. If we don't meet all three of these responsibilities in some way, we may suppress a natural part of our humanness, with all the frustrations that result from suppression; or we can act

'hey charlie...
did you score
last night?'

WELL, OLD BOY, YOU'RE PROBABLY QUITE PROUD OF YOURSELF, AREN'T YOU??
WAS SHE ON THE PILL? DOES SHE HAVE AN IUD? DID YOU REMEMBER YOUR
CONDOMS? OR DID YOU JUST PLAIN FORGET (THE TWO OF YOU) AND TAKE THAT
BIG CHANCE? <u>DON'T</u>!! IF YOU ARE HAVING INTERCOURSE, BE SMART, BE
SAFE, AND USE A RELIABLE CONTRACEPTIVE! HEY, CHARLIE, BIRTH CONTROL
IS YOUR RESPONSIBILITY, TOO!!

HUMAN SEXUALITY CLINIC, UNIVERSITY OF NORTH CAROLINA

FOR INFORMATION, CALL OR COME BY

through instinctual desire, or short-run hedonism, which commonly brings guilt and self-rejection.

Sex is powerful; it is no wonder many have turned to our social institutions—the Home, the Church, the School—to help control sexual behavior. But today we are learning more about the ways in which society can allow the individual to control his own behavior instead of ways his behavior can be controlled by society. For if the individual can assume responsibility for his own life, the energies of society can be directed to more progressive tasks.

The University: A model for action

Because a university campus is a kind of controlled microcosm, it provides us with an excellent model of how society can help the individual to direct his own behavior patterns and answer his needs. At the University of Hawaii, for example, the recognition of students' needs prompted a class poll to evaluate attitudes toward providing birth control for students; 90 percent were in favor. The 1970 senior class voted to start a family planning clinic on campus as its class gift to the university. With tacit approval by the administration, the service began in the Student Health Center under separate administration, and opened as a one-evening-a-week clinic in early 1970. Additional money came from the student government and pharmaceutical companies. Students are charged according to the sliding fee scale of Hawaii Planned Parenthood. Services are available to all students

(regardless of age or marital status), faculty, employees and their families. Obviously this approach would not work for everyone, but it filled the bill for the University of Hawaii.

When students at the University of Maryland were polled, 94 percent felt birth-control services should be available through the University Health Service. Sixty-seven percent of the female students polled said they would certainly use the facilities, provided the service was low in cost and strictly confidential. The survey was a 2 percent sample of all the factions of the university: male/female, sorority/fraternity, graduates/undergraduates, faculty, employees, freshmen through seniors. It was distributed in classes with the permission of sympathetic professors, and a proposal to be presented to the administration was drawn up from the computerized results. Finally, the Chairwoman of the Health Committee recommended the institution of service and a gynecologist was hired for the Health Service staff.

The approach at Kirkland-Hamilton College in New York State is unique—the college requested that Planned Parenthood set up a clinic in the college health center. Needless to say, PP was overjoyed—partly for the chance to try a test case (requests had come from other area colleges previously), and partly because the existing PP clinic was overflowing.

The college donates the space, and appointments are made by the Health Center staff. Planned Parenthood employs a doctor and two nurses while volunteers (students and faculty wives) handle medical records.

CAN SOMEBODY HELP ME?

WE'LL TRY. HERE'S A FEW PEOPLE WHO HAVE AL-
READY CALLED UP FOR HELP:

A FEW GIRLS WHO WERE PREGNANT...AND SOME GUYS
WHO WERE SCARED. A GUY WHO WANTED SOME HAIR ON HIS
CHEST. A MAN WHO WANTED A VASECTOMY. A GUY WHO
BROKE UP WITH HIS GIRLFRIEND. SOME MEN WHO WERE
AFRAID THEY WERE GAY. A WIFE WHOSE HUSBAND WAS TIRED
OF HAVING INTERCOURSE.

CAN WE HELP YOU? MAYBE. BUT WE'LL CERTAINLY
TRY. WE HAVE A PHONE NUMBER YOU CAN CALL AND A PRI-
VATE COUNSELING ROOM FOR TALKS. WE HAVE SHELVES
OF FREE MATERIALS.

GIVE US A CHANCE.

FOR MORE INFORMATION, CALL OR COME BY

HUMAN SEXUALITY CLINIC, UNIVERSITY OF NORTH CAROLINA

group instruction and interviewing. Students are charged the full fee (according to PP fee scales) and contraceptives are sold at the clinic by PP.

Each campus should make its birth-control clinic fit its own particular needs, but students should never aim for, nor be content with, anything less than complete gynecological exams, non-judgmental treatment from all medical personnel, and absolute confidentiality of all records.

Let us assume that you have been appointed to the staff of the newly-formed Office of Human Sexuality, a pilot project to provide for the sexual health, education and counseling needs of the students at the University.

What do you do? First, if the Office of Human Sexuality is to follow through with services to meet these needs, it must consider the University to be not only the administration, but the students, faculty and staff as well. Second, every outlet the university provides must fulfill an important responsibility or provide a necessary duplication or complement of services with another outlet. Projects which are planned for their sensational effects, or which aren't thoroughly thought out or adequately supported, are worse than no projects at all.

Chapter Fourteen: Targets for Change

If you get as far as forming an Office of Human Sexuality on your campus, there are then five major areas in which you can aim for sexual health, education and counseling program development. You can develop sex education materials, try to introduce sexuality into the curriculum, provide for professional sexual health services, set up peer education and counseling services, and put together outreach programs.

Developing Sex Education Materials

Nowhere has the field of sexuality been more explored in the past few years than on the printed page. From dozens to hundreds of pamphlets, books and articles have been published on each aspect of sex, ranging from refined to repulsive, from the scientific to the mythical.

If you are considering materials on sexuality for your school or community, make certain you are not duplicating anything that has already been done adequately by some other individual or organization before you choose to design your own.

One approach to the general reader is "special interest" pamphlets, posters or fliers. These can give some general information about sexuality, and then list community sources of sexual health care, education and counseling. Pamphlets can deal solely with homosexuality, venereal disease, contraception, communication or other topics.

Two examples of special interest booklets are "Birth Control Handbook" and "V.D. Handbook." Single copies of these can be ordered for 25 cents each through P.O. Box 1000, Station G, Montreal 130, Quebec, Canada. These booklets illustrate how factual material might be presented simply and straightforwardly to reach young people.

If you wish to distribute booklets which cover many aspects of sex and sexuality, you have few models from which to work. Most booklets discuss only birth control, abortion, anatomy and physiology of reproduction, and venereal disease.

While these works offer greatly neglected and definitely needed information for those who are having or contemplating sexual intercourse, they can have two negative effects.

First, wide distribution of the booklets can make some young people think that having sexual intercourse is the key to sexual stability, should be sought after by all, and is the outcome of any healthy sexual relationship. This is not usually the position that the authors of the booklets intend to support, but it seems that less secure members of the young community infer it. On campuses where the coed often years ago was ashamed to admit being the only one in her circle of friends having intercourse, today the virgin tends to hide her face.

The second negative effect of such books is that they usually, if indirectly, associate such terms as *love, sex* and *sexuality* only with intercourse. *The Loving Book, Sex Is a Dual Responsibility, How to Take the Worry Out of Being Close, Sex Is Never an Emergency, Between Your Navel and Your Knees* —all are titles of handbooks for young people

Despite the problems involved in relying on booklets to spread information about sex and sexuality, there are a number of those publications available, and some of them are excellent. You might want to have a look at some of the following:

How to Take the Worry Out of Being Close, Marian and Roger Gray, P.O. Box 2822, Oakland, Cal. 94618. 25¢

The Student Guide to Sex on Campus, published by New American Library, sold in bookstores. $1

Birth Control, Abortion and Veneral Disease, Boston University Birth Control Committee, Student Union, 775 Commonwealth Ave., Boston, Mass. 02215. 10¢

Elephants and Butterflies . . . and Contraceptives, ECOS, University of North Carolina, P.O. Box 1055, Chapel Hill, N.C. 27514. $1

A Guide to Contraception and Abortion, Committee on Contraception and Abortion, Medical Center, Durham, N.C. 27006. 25¢

The Boulder Birth Control Handbook, Birth Control Information Commission, UMC 178, University of Colorado, Boulder, Colo. 80302. 25¢

How and Why Not to Have That Baby, Optimum Population, Inc., Charlotte, Vt. 05445. $1

Sex Is Never an Emergency, published by Lippincott, sold in bookstores. 95¢

Venereal Disease, Abortion, Birth Control, Planned Parenthood of Schenectady, 1222 Union St., Schenectady, 1222 Union St., Schenectady, N.Y. 12305. 10¢

Birth Control, Southern Methodist University, Inter Fraternity Council, Dallas, Tex. 75222

Everything You Always Wanted to Know About Birth Control but Were Afraid to Ask, Student Health Center, Colorado State University, Fort Collins, Colo. 80521

The Sperm and Egg Handbook, Community Action Corps, 218 Norton Hall, SUNY Buffalo, Buffalo, N.Y. 14214

How to Have Intercourse Without Getting Screwed, ASUW Woman's Commission, University of Washington, Seattle, Wash. 98195. 25¢

Contraception & VD, Student Health Service, Indiana University, Bloomington, Ind. 47401.

Between Your Navel and Your Knees, Student Association, University of Houston, Houston, Tex. 77040

Sex Is a Dual Responsibility, Student Senate, East Stroudsburg State College, East Stroudsburg, Pa. 18301

Sex Information, Division of Student Affairs, North Carolina State University, Raleigh, N.C. 27607. 10¢

The Loving Book, Red Clay Publishers, Charlotte, N.C. 28002. 75¢

which contain information almost solely relevant to the act of sexual intercourse, most of which can be considered "plumbing" (the basic facts of reproduction, birth control, venereal disease). Sex, sexuality and love can be much more than the act of sexual intercourse. In fact, the day love and sex are reduced to "screwing" will be the day that these words will have little significance in our lives.

What should your booklets contain? One in a series of pamphlets might cover the following points (by no means could all these topics be covered completely in a small booklet, but many can be mentioned briefly, and selected readings can be offered): what is sexuality? how are we sexual? (this covers sex-

Abortion, VD and Birth Control, Student Government Association, University of South Florida, Tampa, Fla. 33620

Medicine for the People, University Health Service, University of Alberta, Edmonton, Alberta, Canada

Birth Control, VD, Abortion, Etc., Student Government Association, University of Maryland, College Park, Md. 20783

Student Sexuality, Health Services Center, Edinboro State College, Edinboro, Pa. 16412

Beyond Eros, Student Government Association, University of Chicago, Chicago, Ill. 60637

Sex is Not a Myth, Anderson Y Center, University of the Pacific, Stockton, Cal. 95204

An Egg and Sperm Handbook, Hudson Health Center, Ohio University, Athens, Ohio 45701

Sex Information for Cornell Students, SECS, Cornell University, Ithaca, N.Y. 14850

Sex Facts for the AU Student, Hotline, American University, Washington, D.C. 20016

1 + 1 =, Student Government Association, State University College of New York at Fredonia, Fredonia, N.Y. 14063

AMATIS, Planned Parenthood League of Massachusetts (with Brandeis University and University of Mass.), 93 Union St., Newton Centre, Mass. 02159

Women's Yellow Pages, The Sanctuary, Inc., 1151 Massachusetts Ave., Cambridge, Mass. 02138. 60¢

Contraceptive Technology 1972, Emory University Family Planning Program, 69 Butler St., S.E., Atlanta, Ga. 30303. 75¢

Birth Control, Venereal Disease, and Pregnancy, Planned Parenthood Association of Cincinnati, Inc. (with University of Cincinnati), 2406 Auburn Ave., Cincinnati, Ohio 45219

Family Planning For Men, Emory University Family Planning Program, 69 Butler St., S.E., Atlanta, Ga. 30303. 20¢

Human Sexual Response-Ability, Student Government Association, Georgetown University, Washington, D.C. 20007. 66¢ (including postage)

Sex, Technology Community Association, MIT, Cambridge, Mass. 02139

Sex Is Nothing to Know Nothing About, Sex Information Center, University of Redlands, Redlands, Cal., 92373

Sex in a Brown Paper Wrapper. Student Committee on Sexuality, Syracuse University, Syracuse, N.Y. 13210

You can obtain any of the above—or find out where to get them—from the College Program, Planned Parenthood—World Population, 810 Seventh Ave., New York, N.Y. 10019.

ual development, maleness, femaleness, sexual identity, our attitudes toward sex, and sex as a natural function); communicating with others, expressing ourselves; how to care for our bodies; variations in sexual attraction (heterosexuality, homosexuality, bisexuality); sexual relationships and responsibilities; physical sexual expression; anatomy and physiol-ogy of reproduction; birth control and abortion; infections and diseases; and sexual myths.

Sexuality in the Curriculum

Introducing sexuality into the curriculum, whether in public schools and colleges or in the community, must be more than an ap-

proach to teaching society's "preventive medicine": how to prevent unwanted pregnancy, how to prevent venereal diseases, how to prevent nonmarital sexual intercourse. It must be more than the antiseptic presentation of the "facts" of sex.

Many conventional sexuality courses contain the basic sex and reproductive information, supplemented with "facts" such as these: nonmarital pregnancy can only end in abortion, forced marriage or disgrace; only bad boys and girls get VD.

The students are left to make their own decisions once they have been "educated." Of course, one of the first things the students discover in these courses is that they are receiving a sterile, biased presentation about a subject they have had experience with, and that they must go elsewhere for the truth. Thus, such sex education courses not only may be useless to the students but can do true damage, in that they may be the first and last chance for the formal educational system to

be trusted by the young with regard to sexual questions and problems.

In the more liberal communities, this approach to sex education is on its way out. However, on some college campuses, the new replacement, designed completely with the typical sexual revolutionary in mind, is just as dangerous. In an editorial in *The SIECUS Report* of November, 1972, Mary Calderone presents these new course designs beautifully:

"Often planned by the office of student personnel and the counseling staff, rarely in consultation with behavioral sciences facilities, much less the students themselves, such a 'course' might consist, as in one case, of a series of eighteen weekly lectures that, in addition to the usuals of birth control, abortion and pregnancy, and homosexuality, also included such supposedly 'with it' topics as vaginal politics, sex and racism, and aspects of male and female liberation.

"Additionally, because this kind of program is built around lecturers . . . who are 'big names' . . . the lectures can be wildly disorganized as to sequence or topics—and decidedly expensive. I would liken this approach to offering an advanced course in calculus to incoming freshmen who have never had a course in basic math."

Now that we have looked at the two extremes, what is the compromise? How should a course in sexuality be designed? Six basic guidelines to teaching such a course will be discussed here. They are: 1) plan your course carefully; 2) allow students to actively participate throughout the course; 3) seek qualified lecturers for special topics; 4) be certain there is constant, visible and empathic leadership; 5) design a meaningful sequence of lectures; and 6) choose adequate course materials.

In planning your course, meet with a small committee of students to "brainstorm" different topics and areas of concern they feel the students are most interested in. Then, as students register for the course, provide them with a questionnaire and the list of topics. Ask them to rank the topics in the order they feel would be most valuable. On the questionnaire, ask for their ideas concerning grades, projects, small group discussions and location and time of the class. Surveying the student needs in this way, and acting on the recommendations, can mean the difference between "meeting the students where we *think* they are" and "meeting the students where they *really* are."

Lay out, on paper, exactly what assumptions you are basing the course on and what the goals of the course are. Then allow the students to make presentations, to be on re-

action panels after certain speakers, to disagree and agree openly in class, and to make creative projects. Incorporate their creative work into the grading system (if you must have one).

Small group discussions are an absolute necessity. Sexuality is an emotion-packed subject and must be handled as such. Students need an opportunity to process new information and share their feelings with their peers, with the help of a trained facilitator. You must understand that this course may be the first time in many students' lives that sex has been dealt with openly, so you should draw up at the outset some assumptions and regulations for the small group interaction.

Your instructor, if you have one, may not feel competent to discuss all aspects of sexuality, so when it's possible or necessary, find other people in the community who have had the experience or training to deal with these topics. For issues that obviously involve two or more possible points of view (for example, abortion), allow all sides an opportunity to speak.

Two basic problems can accrue from courses taught by many lecturers. First, guest lecturers often tend to spend much time "warming up" the audience, and then proceed to duplicate information other speakers have presented. To avoid such repetition, clue your speaker in on what material has already been covered, what the students want and need from him, and what the general feel of the class is (aggressive, completely ignorant of topic, open and receptive, or whatever).

A second problem of guest lecturers is that they too often come on as infallible experts, either in their particular specialties or in the field of sexuality in general. Some students can be overwhelmed by such an approach, so take care that your speakers do not exploit the students in this way.

To avoid the disorganization and conflict that can intrude on some open study groups, your students should always have someone to turn to with questions and problems, for support. A constant, visible, empathic leader who is also knowledgeable about sexuality will provide a focal point for the unity of the group. It should be the responsibility of that leadership to design a meaningful sequence of lectures for the course. Students need to understand themselves before they can truly comprehend the rest of society and how to fit into that society. They need to get a grasp of how and why they think and behave as sexual beings before they can make any positive adjustments to their own sex and sexuality. Thus, any course on sexuality should begin with the individual, not with the way one is *supposed* to behave or what one *should* do to live in society, to prevent problems or to be happy. The sequence of topics for the course can be the same as that in the booklet described on page 100: What is sexuality? How are we sexual? How do we express ourselves and communicate with others? The major difference between the booklet and the course is that in the course the students may react to what is taught and may take a significant role in the teaching and understanding of sexuality.

The course outline should be left as flexible as possible during the last weeks of class, so that needs identified during the course can be met before the end of the semester. No standard course can ever be designed to be used in classes across the country or even by the same community each year, for any course, to keep in touch with those enrolled, must change to fit students' needs. The same criteria apply to the course material you choose. Three books relied on by many college instructors are: *Human Sexual Expression*, by Benjamin A. Kogan (Harcourt Brace Jovanovich, Inc., 1973); *Fundamentals of Human Sexuality*, by Herant A. Katchadourian and Donald T. Lunde (Holt Rinehart and Winston, Inc., 1972); and *Human Sexuality* (Second Edition), by James L. McCary (D. Van Nostrand, 1973). Van Nostrand Company also publishes a Study Guide, an Instructor's Manual and 35mm slides which are designed to supplement *Human Sexuality*. A high school edition by Dr. McCary, called *Human Sexuality: A Course for Young Adults*, is available through American Book Company. Another first-rate book on the subject is *Our Bodies, Our Selves*, which was written and produced by the Boston Women's Health Book Collective, and published by Simon and Schuster ($8.95; $2.95 paper).

In addition to texts, articles with differing opinions on certain aspects of sex should be assigned for the students to read and discuss. For example, many articles are available which present different views on the topics of

nonmarital intercourse, abortion, sexual intercourse without love, homosexuality and, of course, sex education.

The above guidelines were drawn up for a specific course on campus which would deal only with sexuality. Don't forget that sex and sexuality are not objects separate from the other aspects of our life; discussion of them can be incorporated into existing courses within the curriculum, which would give students the perspectives of different educational disciplines. Departments such as sociology, education, health education, social work, religion, anthropology, English, medical studies and nursing all can include the study of sex as it relates to their concerns.

Professional Health Services

Student health services, as well as those in the community, have made substantial and significant changes in their policies and services in an effort to meet the health needs of their patients in the realm of sexuality. But they could go even farther. Some possible suggestions for any public health service follow.

Short training course

Although many health professionals avoid imposing their moral standards on their patients, some don't. Yet mixing judgment with treatment tends to undermine the image of the health service, and interferes with satisfactory health care.

Cases like the following one still happen from time to time. A teenage couple decides to have sexual intercourse, breaking all the religious and family moral codes on which they were raised. Their anxiety about this step is great; their knowledge of contraception is low. After several months of using nothing but prayer, the girl resolves to seek better contraception. With support from her boyfriend she sets up and keeps an appointment at the health service. The physician begins his work-up and continues through a cold, rough pelvic examination with a barrage of comments and questions: Are you getting married? How long have you known him? What would your parents think? Sex is like an expensive wine; you don't guzzle it. Let me tell you an experience I had once. . . .

As the exam and lecture come to an end, the physician suggests: "Why don't you come back in about two weeks after you've thought through this thing? Then I'll discuss putting you on the Pill." The girl, emotionally destroyed by this episode, does not return to a physician until her unwanted pregnancy four months later.

One goal of a staff training course can be to help staff members identify any firmly-held moral positions they have—such as a religious or ethical opposition to abortion—which will prevent them from providing adequate medical care without imposing their value systems at the same time. If they have such positions they should see to it that the patient is referred to someone who can provide the needed care with a more "value-free" approach. (This is better than trying to force the staff to act against their values.)

Many colleges and universities now offer courses in the study of sexuality, some of which might serve as models for you. The following list points out a few outstanding examples; if you want advice or information about how to set up a sexuality course, don't hesitate to write and ask about it.

"Topics in Human Sexuality"
Department of Health Education
School of Public Health
University of North Carolina
Chapel Hill, N.C. 27514

"Human Sexuality"
President's Scholar Program
Southern Illinois University
Carbondale, Ill. 62901

"Human Sexual Behavior"
University Counseling Center
American University

Massachusetts and Nebraska Avenues, N.W.
Washington, D.C. 20016

"Dialogue and Reading in Human Sexuality"
164E. H.P.E. Building
State University of New York
Brockport, N.Y.

"N169: Human Sexuality"
School of Nursing
Duke University
Durham, N.C. 27706

"Human Sexuality"
College of General Studies
Rochester Institute of Technology
Rochester, N.Y. 14623

"Human Sexuality"
University College
Unversity of Florida
Gainesville, Fla. 32601

Women's clinic

Health services can better reach their population if the consumers understand and feel confident in the services offered. One approach to building the confidence of women, as well as to reaching more women than in the past, is to establish and publicize a Women's Clinic within the regular health service. The staff of this clinic should be trained for and sympathetic to the health problems of women.

The Women's Clinic can offer routine and complex gynecological work, including Pap smears and pelvic exams, prescriptions for oral contraceptives, fittings for the IUD and diaphragm; it could also provide contraceptive counseling, problem pregnancy counseling and abortion services or referrals. It could act as a source of medical advice for questions associated with female sexuality, and it might include, as part of its physical plant, a health education room where women can browse through reading materials about their bodies and sexuality, pick up free printed material and view audio-visual resources.

Such a clinic, if it is sufficiently publicized, can have a significant impact on the number of women reached by the service and on the ability of the women to understand their responsibilities to their bodies.

Information about setting up, staffing, and running women's clinics can be obtained from the National Women's Health Coalition, 225 East 35th Street, New York, New York 10016. The Coalition is a network of women's groups involved in educational, medical, counseling, and referral services to women; it

Outstanding Health Service Programs

State University of New York
Brockport, N.Y.
(contraceptive clinic and VD counseling by nursing
students)

Health Service
University of Rochester
Rochester, N.Y.
(contraceptive clinic)

Women's Health Care Clinic
Student Health Service
University of Florida
Gainesville, Fla. 32601
(excellent program for women's health care)

Sex Education, Counseling and Health Program
University Health Service
Princeton University
Princeton, N.J.
(as title implies, offers wide range of services for
students)

Counseling Center
Michigan State University

East Lansing, Mich. 48823
(sexual therapy program for students experiencing
sexual conflicts or dysfunction)

University Health Service
237 East Building
New York University
Washington Square
New York, N.Y. 10003
(birth-control clinic)

Student Health Service
San Fernando Valley State College
Northridge, Cal. 91324
(birth-control and pregnancy counseling service)

Student Health Service
University of Maryland
College Park, Md. 20740
(birth-control clinic)

Family Planning Clinic
University of Hawaii
Honolulu, Hi. 06822
(clinic open to students, faculty and staff)

---

provides counseling on abortion and other gynecological problems to women by telephone or by mail, and it has a whole range of educational materials—pamphlets, slide lecture series, and so on. Such materials could easily be the basis of a collection for the health education room in your women's clinic.

Public Relations

If health services never reach beyond the walls of the buildings in which they are housed, they will miss the opportunity of helping many more people. A Health Educator attached to the health service could publicize new services, write and distribute infor-

mational materials, answer questions from groups and organizations, and provide a source to whom patients can give positive and negative feedback concerning the health service. (All these activities can extend to the realm of sexuality education.) The health educator should openly defend the rights of the patient as a consumer if these rights are violated.

Peer Education and Counseling Services

In the late 1960's, the many crises resulting from the youth drug culture gave rise to the "hotline" and the drop-in crisis center in communities across the country. Today, hotlines and drop-in centers are a common phenomenon; there are "rap houses" and clearinghouses for information on human relations in almost every community. They are usually staffed by a small core of paid personnel, with the assistance of young people trained as volunteer counselors.

Some of these peer counseling centers have extended their services to meet the sexual education and counseling needs of young people in the community, and where such counseling centers do not already exist, some people, especially students, are designing specialized "sexuality information and counseling services" or "birth-control information services."

They use young people as peer counselors, since young people seem to have the spontaneity, the social and cultural proximity to their clients, and the freedom from theoretical framework and professional constraints that this kind of work demands. The peer counselors intervene in crises like problem pregnancies, choice crises or in interpersonal problems, help spread sexuality information to other students via the telephone, personal conferences and group presentations, and serve as a bridge between the student in need of services and the various medical and mental health resources available in the community. They can also serve such miscellaneous functions as describing routine procedures (the insertion of an IUD), illuminating institutional policies, and commenting on the competence and attitudes of professionals (suggesting who will give a moral lecture

about nonmarital intercourse).

If you're thinking of setting up a sexuality counseling center, you should first consider the size of the population to be served. It would be senseless to design a large information and counseling service staffed forty hours a week with highly trained volunteers if your campus population is 4,000 students or less. The most effective means of reaching a small community is to create educational teams, which can plan and implement discussion groups and presentations to dormitory students, sororities, fraternities, classes and campus organizations. They can also be the focal points for working on campus policy changes, development of courses and design of books. Larger communities, of course, are apt to support a more complete counseling and referral service. If your budget is small but the need is great, don't let that stop you. One campus group serviced 1000 problems on a $150 budget.

Don't guess what those in your community might need—*survey* those needs by talking with the consumers themselves, as well as with the professionals who work with those you wish to help. Some communities may want only birth-control information, while others may be looking for a place where they can share their feelings on a one-to-one basis or in group sessions with their peers.

Your organization should provide either a unique service or a necessary duplication or complement to an already existing service. If your student health service is providing adequate birth control information and care,

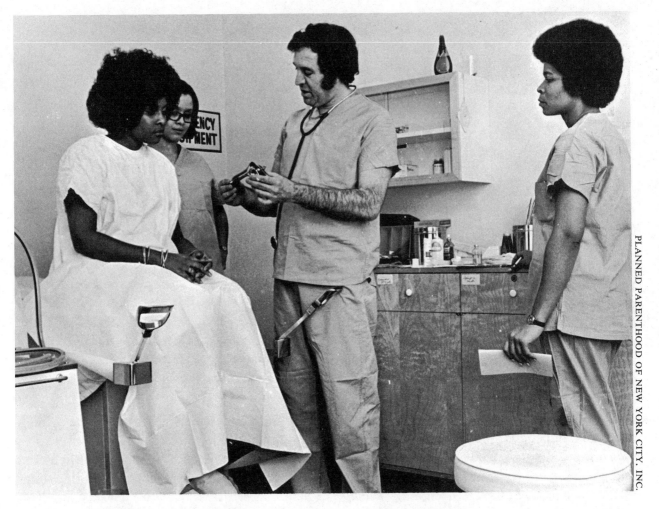

What sort of caseload will a sexuality counseling service have to carry? Here is a record of the cases handled by Human Sexuality Information and Counseling Service, University of North Carolina, from October 18, 1971 through October 14, 1973.

	Number of Cases	Percent of total
Contraceptive information and referral	1122	26%
General information	596	14
Pregnancy information and referral	514	12
Abortion information and referral	479	11
VD, other infections	400	9
Interpersonal/marital problems	329	8
Research	218	5
Physiology/sexual techniques	201	5
Homosexuality	154	4
Sexual inadequacies	157	4
Prank/crank calls	58	1
Programming	56	1
Total	4284	

Average number of cases handled per week = 65

you may not need to supplement it. But if the health service does little publicity or offers no counseling on contraception, a peer counseling service may bridge the gap.

Organizing and coordinating your service is no easy task. Operating with an all-volunteer staff comprised mainly of students means a high turnover rate and probably annual or semi-annual orientation and training. Co-ordinating with professional services is a tough and sometimes highly sensitive job, and your leaders must be dedicated, knowledgeable, skilled individuals in touch with the feelings of young people.

To insure coordination with the professional community and to assist the group in increasing its skills, your service should work directly with one or more professionals who can provide advice in meetings, assist in staff training, serve as liason between your group and the professional services, and answer questions or problems too difficult for the student counselors to handle. These will crop up from time to time, and you should know enough not to try to cope with them. Your educators or counselors can only handle cases that they feel trained enough and comfortable enough to accept. Know your limitations. If your training program only taught sex education, don't allow your students to be considered "counselors." At the end of training, let your students test themselves on their knowledge. If they are weak in one area, continue that training. Let them role-play cases; it's good practice, and the most effective measure of how well they will function with the real thing.

The best way to train educator-counselors is to choose your staff, and then train them. This avoids wasting the time and aspirations of trainees who don't make the grade. If you have a great number of volunteers, you will have to resort to an application form to screen out some. Or you might ask them one question: Why have you chosen this time in your life to become involved in this type of service?

The most effective screening, though, is to have one applicant act as a "counselor" and one as "counselee," with another as an observer, and have the three improvise a role-playing situation. In one such situation, the "counselee" might be told: "You are a female virgin who is down on herself because she is the 'only one left on the hall who's not on the Pill.' You are feeling you might as well get it over with and have intercourse with your boyfriend." The counselee then plays this role and the counselor responds accordingly. After five or ten minutes a trainer ends the situation, and all three applicants can discuss the experience. Then all three rotate roles. Trainers can discuss the weaknesses of the applicants among themselves and watch for improvements throughout the screening. After a sufficient number of role-playing situations, the trainers select as trainees those applicants whom they consider to be the most responsible, empathic and sensitive counselors. The more that counseling skills are found intrinsically within your applicants, the better your service will be for it. If you accept a responsible person into your service, you know that if he becomes involved with a case too difficult to handle, he will be able to admit the problem and refer his counselee to someone more qualified.

Your initial training program can be as short as twenty hours long (a few hours each night) with special education sessions at your regular meetings, but it should focus as much on the skills needed to cope with a specific situation as on the information needed to deal with it. The Human Sexuality Information and Counseling Service at the University of North Carolina handles cases in twelve different categories, from crank calls to VD information to birth control referral. The breakdown of their cases, on the opposite page, can indicate what topics would be most valuable in training.

Campus Information and/or Counseling Services

The following universities and colleges are just a few of the many that are beginning to provide sex information or counseling services by peers and may be able to help you in your efforts:

Human Sexuality Information and Counseling
  Service
Box 51, Carolina Union Building
University of North Carolina
Chapel Hill, N.C. 27514

Human Sexuality Services
Southern Illinois University
Carbondale, Ill. 62901

Birth Control Information Committee
Student Government
Monroe Community College
Rochester, N.Y. 14263

Sex Education Committee
University of Rochester
Rochester, N.Y. 14600

Sex Information Center
Associated Students
University of Redlands
Redlands, Cal. 92373

Abortion Information Dissemination Group
University of Florida
Gainesville, Fla. 32601

Office of Human Sexuality
Bucknell University
Lewisburg, Pa. 17837

Birth Control Center
Clark University
Worcester, Mass. 01610

Sexuality Information Service
University of Massachusetts
Boston, Mass. 02100

EROS
School of Education
Boston University
Boston, Mass. 02100

Sexuality Information Service
Wellesley College
Wellesley, Mass. 02181

Counselors Committee on Human Sexuality
University of Virginia
Charlottesville, Va. 22903

Women's Health and Information Service
Central Michigan University
Box 110, Warriner Hall
Mount Pleasant, Mich. 48859

Birth Control and Information Center
Colgate University
Rochester, N.Y. 14620

Outreach programs

Even if students on your campus don't immediately come to you of their own accord, you can carry your quiet revolution to them. You can create all sorts of small and large outreach projects on your campus, from something as seemingly small as a "Dear Abby" type column in your school paper to answer sexual questions, to something as ambitious as a one- or two-day sexuality program

with educational movies, displays, workshops and games. Or you can organize a short training course on sexuality for the student dormitory counselors, have a campus speaker series, begin some consciousness-raising groups, encounter groups or small group discussion meetings, get the library to stock up on some sexuality books and journals, or design dorm presentations on birth control.

It only takes some imagination and a look

ABORTION

IF YOU'VE MISSED A PERIOD, AND THINK YOU
MAY BE PREGNANT, DON'T HESITATE TO HAVE A
PREGNANCY TEST.   THE TEST CAN BE PERFORMED
AS LITTLE AS TWO WEEKS AFTER THE MISSED
PERIOD.   NO FEE IS CHARGED AT THE STUDENT
HEALTH SERVICE.   NON-STUDENTS CAN BE TESTED
AT THE ENDOCRINE LAB OF N. C. MEMORIAL
HOSPITAL FOR $4.00. (ASK FOR A UCG - urinary
choriogonadotropin test).

SINCE ABORTIONS ARE BEST PERFORMED BETWEEN
THE 7th AND 10th WEEK OF PREGNANCY, ACT
NOW!!

DO YOU NEED SOMEONE TO TALK TO?   WOULD YOU
LIKE THE DETAILS ABOUT ABORTIONS?   ...WHERE
ABORTIONS CAN BE OBTAINED?   ...THE PRICES...
THE PROCEDURES?

FOR MORE INFORMATION, CALL OR COME BY

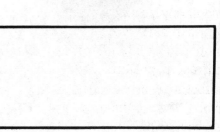

HUMAN SEXUALITY CLINIC, UNIVERSITY OF NORTH CAROLINA

Information, Materials and Sources

If you want to know more about how to expand sexual health, educational or counseling services on your campus, try some of the following:

Organizations

Youth and Student Affairs
Planned Parenthood—World Population
810 Seventh Avenue
New York, N.Y. 10019

Publishes *Getting It Together*, a newsletter for those involved in sexuality programs for young people. Offers good contacts.

Sex Information and Education Council of the United States (SIECUS)
1855 Broadway
New York, N.Y. 10023

Acts as a clearing house for programs, provides study guides, conducts training programs.

American Association of Sex Educators and Counselors
815 15th St., N.W.
Washington, D.C. 20005

National and regional training workshops on sexuality education and counseling. Quarterly newsletter.

Journals and Newsletters

Journal of Sex Research
c/o Society for the Scientific Study of Sex, Inc.
Suite 1104
12 East 41st St.
New York, N.Y. 10017
$12.50 per volume (4 issues per year)

Archives of Sexual Behavior
Plenum Press
227 West 17th St.
New York, N.Y. 10011
$26.00 per year (institutional), $16.00 per year (individual)

Medical Aspects of Human Sexuality
Hospital Publications, Inc.
18 East 48th St.
New York, N.Y. 10017
$20.00 per year

Sexology
Sexology Corporation
200 Park Ave. South
New York, N.Y. 10003
$5.00 per year

Focus on the Family
E. C. Brown Center for Family Studies
University of Oregon
1802 Moss St.
Eugene, Ore. 97403
bi-monthly, no charge

Say It So It Makes Sense
Institute for Family Research and Education
760 Ostrom Ave.
Syracuse, N.Y. 13210
quarterly, $25.00 for 2 years

Family Planning Perspectives
Planned Parenthood Federation of America, Inc.
515 Madison Ave.
New York, N.Y. 10023
quarterly, no charge

Journal of Marriage and the Family and
The Family Coordinator
National Council on Family Relations
1219 University Ave. S.E.
Minneapolis, Minn. 55414
quarterlies, $15.00 each per year

SIECUS Report
The Sex Information and Education Council of the United States
1855 Broadway
New York, N.Y. 10023
bi-monthly, $7.00 per year

Sex News
P. K. Houdek
7140 Oak
Kansas City, Mo. 64114
monthly, $2.00 per year

Audio-Visual Materials and Distributors

*Family Life: Literature and Films, an annotated
    bibliography*
Minnesota Council on Family Relations
    Minneapolis, Minn. 1972
1219 University Avenue S.E., Minneapolis,
    Minn. 55414. $3.65

*Sex Education on Film: a guide to visual aids and
    programs*
by Singer, Laura J., and Buskin, Judith
Teachers College Press
Columbia University
1234 Amsterdam Ave.
New York, N.Y. 10027

Film Resources for Sex Education.
Sex Information and Education Council of the
    United States (SIECUS)
1855 Broadway
New York, N.Y. 10023

Multi-Media Resource Center
Room 439, 340 Jones St.
San Francisco, Cal. 94102

Perennial Education, Inc.
1825 Willow Rd.
P. O. Box 236
Northfield, Ill. 60093

Picture Films Distribution Corporation
43 West 16th St.
New York, N.Y. 10011
(films—*Lucy, Better by Choice . . . Than by
    Chance*)

Department of Education and Social Concern
Unitarian Universalist Association
25 Beacon St.
Boston, Mass. 02108
(multimedia—*About Your Sexuality*; record/film-
    strip—*The Invisible Minority*)

Teacher Training Aids
27 Harvey Dr.
Summit, N.Y. 07901
(slides—*Breaking the Language Barrier*—excellent)

Texture Films, Inc.
1600 Broadway
New York, N.Y. 10019
(films—*About Sex, A Three Letter Word for Love,
    How About You*)

EDCOA Productions
520 South Dean St.
Englewood, N.J. 07631

Washington University School of Medicine
Department of Illustration
4950 Audubon Ave.
St. Louis, Mo. 63110
(slides—*Human Sexual Response*)

Books

Abramson, Beth. *Right Now It's a Love Trip: A
Handbook for the Development of Contraceptive
and Pregnancy Counselling Programs for Teenagers.* Planned Parenthood of Alameda—San Francisco. 476 West MacArthur Blvd., Oakland, Cal.,
94609. 1972.

Belliveau, Fred and Richter, Lin. *Understanding
Human Sexual Inadequacy.* New York: Bantam,
1970.

Brecher, Ruth and Edward. *An Analysis of Human
Sexual Response.* New York: New American
Library, 1966.

Broderick, Carlfred B. and Bernard, Jessie. *The Individual, Sex, and Society: A SIECUS Handbook for Teachers and Counselors*. Baltimore: The Johns Hopkins Press, 1969.

Lehrman, Nat. *Masters and Johnson Explained*. Chicago: Playboy Press Book, 1970.

Mace, David R. *Abortion—The Agonizing Decision*. Nashville: Abington Press, 1972.

Masters, William and Johnson, Virginia. *Human Sexual Inadequacy*. Boston: Little, Brown, 1970.

Masters, William and Johnson, Virginia. *Human Sexual Response*. Boston: Little, Brown, 1966.

Peel, John and Potts, Malcolm. *Textbook of Contraceptive Practice*. London: Cambridge University Press, 1970.

Rubin, I. and L. A. Kirkendall (eds.). *Sex In the Adolescent Years: New Directions in Guiding and Teaching Youth*. New York: Association Press, 1969.

Schiller, Patricia. *Creative Approach to Sex Education and Counseling*. New York: Association Press, 1973.

Wilson, Robert R. *Contraceptive Education: A Self-instructional Course*. Carolina Population Center, 500 Pittsboro St., Chapel Hill, N.C. 27514. 1973. (booklet)

Wilson, Robert R. *Introduction to Sexual Counseling*. Carolina Population Center, 500 Pittsboro St., Chapel Hill, N.C. 27514. 1973. (booklet)

Wilson, Robert R. (ed.). *Problem Pregnancy and Abortion Counseling*. Saluda, N.C.: Family Life Publications, 1973.

at your present situation to get started. For instance, the Sex Information Center at the University of Redlands (Redlands, California 92373) designed a "Sexuality Week" and a "VD Week" for the students on their campus. Both met with great success. The General Student Senate at the University of Maine (Orono, Maine 04473) set up a $5000 abortion loan fund so that women could afford to travel to New York for abortions if necessary. Whatever the needs of your campus, you can help to provide the services essential for better sexual health, education and counseling. You—and your campus—can only benefit.

Part Four: Action for High School Students

Chapter Fifteen: Education

If you're a high school student and concerned about the population problem—what it involves, what it means—you may be wondering how you can fit into the picture. After all, your resources, in time and money, are limited; you can hardly influence an election campaign, take a population lawsuit through the courts, or set up a legislative lobbying office—but take heart.

Consciousness Raising

Action does not always require a cast of thousands of outfitted troops, marshalled and meshing like a synchronized motor. Some effective activities—particularly those aimed at raising the consciousness of your audience—can be done alone, without extensive resources. Many everyday opportunities can be used to stimulate thinking about population. Consciousness raising, unlike education, doesn't necessarily try to teach people about population. Rather, it focuses the attention of your audience on population as an important dynamic in their lives. Who is your audience? It can be found almost anywhere—school newspaper readers, classmates, supermarket shoppers, people standing in line.

Taking Advantage of Where You're At

Judy Johnson, a high school senior and valedictorian of her graduating class in Sedro Woolley, Washington, had to give that inspirational valedictorian address. She was also working within a school policy which stated that all seniors giving commencement speeches must have their speeches cleared by the administration. The policy did *not* say that speeches, once cleared, couldn't be rewritten.

Judy wanted to say something about population in a powerful way. And she decided that her proposal probably wouldn't pass administration inspection. She wanted to unsettle rather than pacify the audience. She did. Her final speech contained a lot of talk about the necessity of change, moral and physical, in order to insure a brighter and liveable tomorrow. In the midst of her "inspiring" speech, she was interrupted by a co-conspirator in the audience, who said, "But Judy, you're missing the whole point when you talk about change and a better future if you don't deal with the threat of population growth."

This is obviously a dramatic example—not easily or readily repeatable—but it shows how to use a fairly improbable existing situation in a creative and potentially effective way. It's also a good example of consciousness-raising activity. Judy was not trying to help people understand the dynamics of population growth as much as she was trying once again to bring it to their attention as a dynamic force in their lives.

To focus the attention of a whole community on population requires more planning, more marshalling of your troops. For example, interesting and easily accessible activities can be used to attract press and radio coverage. ZPG high school and college students spent a crowded weekend in beautiful downtown Minneapolis to focus attention on international population and development prob-

Members of the Seattle, Washington chapter of Zero Population Growth have put together a flyer about overcrowding which they hand out to people standing in lines. Couldn't you ask the same questions?

How Much Time Do You Spend in These Lines?

☐ Supermarket

☐ Movie theater

☐ Ferry line

☐ Restaurant

☐ Stores

☐ Traffic jam

☐ Auto licensing

☐ Voting

☐ Bank

☐ Football stadium

. . . or just looking for a parking space?

This time is the direct cost to you of overcrowding!

Even if we haven't actually run out of space yet, even if we still haven't had to fill in Lake Washington and Puget Sound to make room for more subdivisions, we're all feeling the effects of overpopulation right now—when we find that the campgrounds are all full on a summer weekend, for example.

And lines aren't the *only* problem caused by population growth!

There are lots of others!

☐ Pollution

☐ Urban problems

☐ Crime

☐ War

☐ Overcrowded classrooms

☐ Declining quality of life

☐ Increasing restrictions on individual liberty

☐ High taxes

☐ Overcrowded recreational areas

Halting Population Growth Won't Solve Any of These Problems—But It Will Make It Possible to Solve Them!

Population growth means we need:

☐ more highways

☐ more suburbs

☐ more schools

☐ more sewers

☐ more power plants or dams

☐ more hospitals

☐ MORE EVERYTHING

(which means more taxes to pay for it all).

As the Red Queen says in *Alice in Wonderland,* "Now, *here*, you see, it takes all the running you can do, to keep in the same place."

lems. Remember old movies about the marathons in store fronts? This program was a marathon with a message: sixty-four people in a store front, with fifteen square feet for

each person, and 650 calories allotted for each to consume during the weekend. The planners had decided space and calorie allotments from information in a *Time* magazine article about conditions in Calcutta. The original and primary purpose of the "be in" was street theater—publicity for ZPG and another word about the threat of population growth. But much personal learning also occurred among the participants. Everyone had to keep a diary of the weekend, and these diaries relate very interesting accounts of tired, irritated people waiting in lines, suffering from lack of sleep, energy and privacy —people in a zoo.

The dynamics of the weekend were in some ways manipulated before the fact. Decisions were to be made democratically. Participants were of various ages. But decisions about equal apportionment of space and food were decided by the group members on the scene. They also decided whether to admit latecomers to the experiment. And they even had to make rules for use of the one bathroom.

The "be in" had lots of press coverage. Group members had contacted all feature writers in the area who had indicated an interest in conservation. Radio spot announcements were used prior to the big weekend. And the subject matter was interesting and newsworthy. Street theater is always good for audience appeal; it's fun and requires an immediate response. It demands more from the onlooker than TV, a pamphlet or a book.

The store front was donated. ZPG people found a store which hadn't been rented in a year—dirty and lonely. They agreed to clean the building and to leave the FOR RENT sign in the window. So, as the window with all its population messages was beamed into the living rooms of Minneapolis, so was the owner's rent plea.

As it turned out, they all lived happily ever after. Participants went home. The owner rented his building. ZPG got enough new memberships to pay for the food and other expenses incurred by the weekend happenings. And group members felt that they had graphically relayed a population threat to the citizens of Minneapolis.

Education

The word *education* conjures forth visions of structured learning environments, textbooks, teachers, desks, research, etc. However, much education is the result of simple observation and everyday living experience. Nonetheless, working for educational change in schools can be difficult. Here, allies and legitimization become most important. Having all the students in the world behind an idea does no good if parents, teachers and administrators are not involved.

For some class subjects, however, you or an outside agency can logically and effectively serve in some of the teaching roles. Sex education may be one such subject (an area where teachers are particularly fearful of treading). The legitimization and help available from organizations like Planned Parenthood can be invaluable.

Vicki Bearman, a high school student in San Pedro, California, taught contraceptive information classes in her school, and was then invited to teach similar classes at other area schools. Reaching this goal was not

---

What's it like to be transported to the year 2000? High school students in Minneapolis ZPG tried the experiment, spending a weekend in a crowded storefront, with fifteen square feet and 650 calories allotted to each person for the whole two days. Here's part of the diary of one of the participants in the Minneapolis Marathon:

Saturday, 3:00 p.m. I'm becoming very lethargic —I don't want to read, I don't want to sing or play the guitar, I don't want to write in this damn journal, I don't even want to talk to people anymore. . . . It's by no means unbearable yet, though I'm going to feel differently if I can't sleep again to-night. . . . You know what makes this situation so artificial? We *know* we're getting out of here in another 31 hours. We *know* that we'll have food soon—by the year 2000, these opportunities will *not* be open. I'm really tired of having to walk over people, and having people walk over me. . . . I'm so damned hungry that I can't cope with some of the things that happen. . . . *Saturday, 6:30 p.m.* We discovered that we have enough fruit to give everybody an orange tonight—Hurray! It makes me happy—strangely enough—to be able to give everybody a little extra. Maybe 'cause little things have become so tremendously important.

---

easy, but Vicki finally won through. She had been participating in Planned Parenthood sexuality and contraception rap sessions, and therefore had knowledge of the subjects as well as an expanded awareness of her contemporaries' needs. She asked to see the course outline for the health education classes within her high school, and after reviewing the outline and talking with the instructors she learned that, although sex education was included in the course, no mention was made of contraception. Vicki suggested that such information should be in the course. At this point, she was sent to talk with the principal, who wasn't convinced that the inclusion of contraceptive information was either proper or necessary. Our heroine left the principal's office, exasperated but undaunted, to talk with students.

The word soon got around that Vicki was trying to document the importance of making contraceptive information readily available within her school. She was keeping a count of students who were having sexual intercourse but not using contraceptives, and of students who had abortions. The stakes were high. If the proposal were accepted it would mean the availability of vital information for students now, and for younger brothers and sisters later. Fellow students came to Vicki to tell her how much they supported what she was doing. They also volunteered information for her lists. (Of course all information sources were kept confidential.)

The principal was astounded when Vicki took the figures to him. He agreed to let Vicki teach the class (the teachers' initial excuses had been that they didn't know enough about contraceptives to teach about them) if she would send a letter to all parents describing the need for the class and her qualifications to teach it. She also had to ask them to respond negatively if they didn't want their child to participate.

The process described here in a few sentences was a long and often discouraging one,

but Vicki's initiative demonstrated the need, demand, acceptability and credibility of providing contraceptive information within regular classroom situations. Her project has served not only to provide information now, but as a pilot for future health education classes.

There are other ways to bring the population problem into the schools. Individual students in a couple of ecology classes in Lebanon. New Hampshire requested that, as part of their reports on population, Planned Parenthood staff people be invited to speak to the entire class. This was an easy request to fill; it involved (in each instance) one student, one class, one teacher who was already concerned about the environment, one administrator and one Planned Parenthood speaker. On the basis of good class experiences and an establishment of credibiilty, the word spread, and other classes began to ask for speakers. Administrators and a school board member (or two) sat in on a class (or two). It was a small scale program, and everybody was happy.

Then, because of the number of requests that the Planned Parenthood people were receiving, they began to meet with and train teachers so that they could assume responsibility for the same information within their own classrooms.

And then some work-study students chose Planned Parenthood for their placement; they received credit for doing community education (working with libraries and making posters), and serving as in-school representatives of Planned Parenthood (providing a ready resource for other students). And *then* Planned Parenthood asked for and was granted a meeting room in each of the three Lebanon high schools, in which to hold two-hour weekly rap sessions during school time. Because of the rapport established with teachers and administrators, students were free to drop in whenever they had something to ask or talk about. Subjects ranged from sexuality and contraception, to social hassles, to world population problems.

It's still going on. Students come and students go. And the rap sessions remain, providing opportunities for dialogue and questioning.

Assemblies, Clubs, Libraries

Changing the curriculum or getting a course adopted can sometimes have lasting effects. Easier but more short-term activities include special assemblies or displays. For assemblies and special occasions, guest speakers are readily available—and are often flattered to be asked. Here, a high school student from Portland, Oregon recounts the story of her adventures with Population Studies Week:

"I wanted to do something to raise the general consciousness of students of the school (and hopefully the community through them) about the implications of over-population . . . I wanted to bring up the questions of whether population was a problem, how much of a problem and what could and should be done.

"We decided to have a Population Studies Week, modeling it after a very successful week of films and artwork produced to introduce students to the Performing Arts, called Performing Arts Week. That is, we thought our name would suggest the same type of multi-media and seminar approach of the PAW, and we decided to similarly include seminars, speakers and films. We were lucky in that the ZPG people we got in touch with, a group from the local medical school, were very enthusiastic and volunteered their services as speakers and discussion leaders. They also suggested a good movie that was made by a physician in Washington that talked about population and methods of birth control. We knew from the start that we were going to have trouble with the administration. But the fact that the film focused on nude genitals of both males and females and that there was a section showing the insertion of an IUD was sure to cause *more* trouble. Which brings us to our next topic, selling the project to the administration.

"First of all, calling it Population Studies Week was a help because supposedly you can STUDY anything. They didn't want us to draw any conclusions and they wanted to make sure that the ZPG people came as medical students and not as proponents of zero population growth. They decided that the program had to be approved as a project of the social studies department. Luckily we had a good guy in the Social Studies department who thought the idea was a good one and would help us. Next, the rest of the department decided that if we had med students known to be ZPG there, we had better invite some Right to Life people to balance the slate. We answered with their own argument by reminding them that it was not a partisan debate and that the

Changing the Curriculum

Even more difficult than adapting the content of a class or course is changing the curriculum. Yet it can be done, and here are some cases which have had success.

Four work-study students from high schools in the Boulder, Colorado area spent one year (September–July), working three hours each afternoon with a local education organization (Social Sciences Education Consortium), to produce a "schoolbook," a "tool" which could be used by other students to de-velop their own course on the environment. (If you want to see a copy, write: Social Sciences Education Consortium, Educational Resources Center, 855 Broadway, Boulder, Colo. 80302.) The students were recruited via a newspaper article and announcements in the area high schools. An initial meeting was held for interested students who then went through an application-interview process. Students received different credits from their individual schools, and were paid $1.75 an hour for extra time spent. This is an example med students were going to present facts and hold open forums so it was not a matter of representing sides. They finally said O.K. to that. Then they insisted on seeing the movie before we showed it. So I and two teachers and the Principals had a preview. I thought the film was good, healthy and innocuous enough in that it presented facts and did it nicely. The administration thought that it would shock kids who would in turn go home and tell their parents about the awful pornography that the high school was sponsoring and so on. We finally got permission to show the movie with the provision that it be only open to classes going with a teacher who could subsequently deal with anyone's feelings about it and make sure everyone understood that the school was taking no position on birth control.

"As it turned out, we had a pretty well planned and executed week, with each day devoted to a different aspect, such as 'Is Population a Problem,' 'What Can Be Done,' etc. People responded very well and the sessions were well attended. I wished that classes had been suspended because only the same group of interested students always turned up. The administration got a little flak but they didn't pass it on to me so I never heard what the complaints were. Our school paper gave us a pretty flattering article and editorial.

"Anyway, to summarize, I'll list my recommendations to other interested high school students:
1) Have it be population STUDIES rather than indoctrination . . . the facts speak for themselves and otherwise no administration will buy it.
2) Get as many segments of the school as possible involved in planning and execution . . . such as biology classes studying ecology, urban studies classes, health classes, etc. The sessions will then have a better quality of study (preparation) as well as approval and attendance.
3) Use the media—slides, films, posters—and have speakers and discussions. The more variety in your presentation, the better.
4) It may be possible to get funds as a class project or a department project; you need money for movies and speakers' honorariums.
5) To make the thing come off smoothly takes a lot of thinking of *how* and *when* to present the project to the administration as well as a lot of planning and work if you do get it approved . . . to make it a memorable experience for the students."

of using the system of school and credits to do creative things. It's getting where *you* want to be and doing what *you* want to do. It's accepting a lot of responsibility for your own education, and that's not easy. But the surface has only been scratched. Students are just beginning to see how they can use existing opportunities to create their own learning/living situations. Crossing tracks to gain experience in personal areas or interest can also build "points" with college admissions people—more and more colleges are looking for students who can take responsibility for their own education. If you want to initiate a work-study program in your school, and need some back-up, have a look at *Free to Learn*: *Unlocking and Ungrading American Education*, by John Henry Martin and Charles H. Harrison (Prentice-Hall, 1972, $2.45). This is a very quotable book for use with school counselors, administrators, parents, and so on. The authors talk about how work-study is or can be an educationally sound, valuable experience for *all* students.

Sometimes the initiative for changing the curriculum will come from the faculty. One teacher at South San Francisco High School saw the need for education about human sexuality, and began to include material about it within his regular social studies classes. This wasn't enough, so he brought together a group of students he thought would be interested, and proposed that they work to change the curriculum schoolwide. In the meantime, they were to educate themselves so that they could personally serve as resources. It sounded like a good idea—a chance not only to learn more personally, but also to provide an important service to other students. The group members studied and talked, printed a list of their names and phone numbers, and spread the word about their availability and ability to answer questions. Thus far, the official curriculum hasn't changed, but lots of questions are being answered *now*; and the students are still working on the longer-range goal of institutionalizing the availability of sex information at South San Francisco High.

While many education programs have been started in high schools on the initiative of individual students or teachers, don't rule out the possibility that an affiliate of one of the national population organizations might help you get a program started. One such program was started in Los Angeles when the Planned Parenthood branch there hired a full-time staff member to work with students in rap sessions, putting together radio talk shows and organizing school meetings. The resulting group, called YES, also held a poster contest to generate some good population-related art work.

Clubs and Libraries

In some cases it isn't possible to get courses in population problems or sex education; yet, by circumventing the rules and using the existing system, you *can* make a difference. Some high school students in the Oakland, California area decided to take the responsibility for their sex education into their own hands, since legal restrictions on sex education within the curriculum have caused many schools in California to ignore the issue. But students are allowed to participate in duly recognized activities after school hours on school property, and that's the opening. A number of students have formed extracurricular study groups with the purpose of increasing their understanding of human sexuality, contraception, and so on. The groups meet during activity periods after school; they schedule speakers, discussion of specific topics or just rap sessions. They also share and discuss relevant books, pamphlets, magazine articles, and so on.

Another way to get new material into the school—if not into the classroom—is to work with your school librarian. Libraries are more effective than you might think. School libraries are more heavily funded (by the Secondary and Elementary Education Act) than most individual classrooms, and public libraries have had funds specifically allotted to them (under the Environmental Education Act) to develop environmental resource centers. See if you can get your librarian to put some of these funds into a shelf of books on population and sex-related problems. Although some librarians are protective parental figures, most are dedicated to making information accessible to everyone who asks; working with such a librarian to develop a "population bookshelf" might be a good beginning program for your environmental/population group.

Chapter Sixteen: Services

The list of organizations (Planned Parenthood chapters, Public Health, Free Clinics, etc.) offering hassle-free, confidential services to minors is growing. However, the number of organizations and doctors who are still hiding behind the law (see legality of services to minor arguments, p. 52), or who are not willing to accept minors, unmarried people or whatever in a non-judgmental way, is still large enough to discourage students from seeking out the services they need. The search can be a long drawn-out process, and often at its end some "well-meaning" clinic person will telephone parents to inform them of what's going on. To lessen those threats, some students have compiled lists of local clinics where minors can receive confidential contraceptive, VD and abortion services. Some of these lists have found their way into the more general contraceptive handbooks.

The lists are easy to draw up. In New York, the High School Women's Coalition telephoned all the organizations providing family-planning services to ask if they would serve minors—a fairly straightforward approach—and published a list of hassle-free clincs, hospitals and information services in English and Spanish.

High school students in Laguna Beach, California are honoring a tried and true custom—using bathroom walls and other easily accessible places to spread the word. A small pamphlet (folded to fit inconspicuously into pockets or wallets) entitled "Because You Care" contains a brief description of various birth control methods, a word about VD and lots of local telephone numbers for birth-control services, pregnancy testing, abortion and adoption referrals. The pamphlets are placed in envelopes which are stuck to walls with double-sided masking tape. And the message, along with the specific details, is an old one, dating from 1859. It comes from John Stuart Mill's *On Liberty*: "The fact itself of causing the existence of a human being is one of the most responsible actions in the range of human life. To understand this responsibility, to bestow life which may either be a curse or a blessing, unless the being on whom it is to be bestowed will have at least the ordinary chances of desirable existence, is a crime against that being."

Parents

Parents are possibly the most hassled and most confused of people about the issue of their children's sexuality. Because they're parents, and sometimes protective, they don't want their children to be fathers or mothers too soon. Parents are sometimes afraid to talk about the issue of sexuality and contraception, and often wish it just didn't exist. But they also have the potential of being powerful allies in the struggle to establish confidential contraceptive services for minors—because they have concern for their offspring, and because they often don't know how to handle the issue themselves and would like to turn it over to someone else. When parents organize to demand services, school systems are very susceptible. In Balboa, California, a group of parents, along with a couple of public health nurses, have opened up the high school nurse's office so that a doctor can do pelvic examinations and prescribe contraceptives under school auspices. This kind of program is not likely to happen in many schools for a long time (if ever). But it does demonstrate "parent power."

In order for parents to be able to move, they need to know what's going on. Students can provide a lot of back-up information. How many pregnancies, abortions, VD occurences happened last year among students in School A? How many students are having sexual intercourse and how many are using contraceptives? Obviously, students can get this kind of information more easily than their parents can—especially if fellow-students know that the proposed plan involves education and services for themselves and their successors.

Putting It Together

If you want to get birth-control and other population-related services set up in your school or community, the best way to convince those in authority that you mean business is to put together a comprehensive and carefully thought-out program that outlines the needs for these services and shows how you think they ought to work. Some high school students in New York City, who got together as the Coalition for Relevant Sex Education, did just that; they researched and wrote up a proposal entitled *Birth Control and Venereal Disease Information and Refer-*

ral Project in New York City Public High Schools, working with a staff member from the city's Human Resources Administration as well as with a graduate student from one of the city's schools of social work. They presented the proposal, along with a petition signed by 9,000 students that demanded the program as outlined, and after long questioning by school board members and much politicking by officials, the program was adopted.

What the Student Coalition for Relevant Sex Education had done, primarily, was to show clearly the need for the services they asked for. In a brief introduction to their proposal they described how ignorance of birth control and related matters led to confusion, injury and sometimes death for their classmates. They cited statistics (in 1969, more than 4,000 babies were born out of wedlock to girls aged fifteen to seventeen; more than 6,000 were born to girls aged eighteen to nineteen; in 1970, almost 11,000 babies were born out of wedlock to girls under the age of fifteen) and described the numbers of cases in which high school students were forced to turn to illegal abortions—some with fatal results. To combat these gruesome facts, the Coalition was proposing its program, which would make facts on birth control available to those who wanted them, and would provide appropriate referrals for students who needed them. First, they proposed that existing school courses in "Family Living" be strengthened to include information on contraception, and that these courses be taught at the ninth-grade level (not the eleventh-grade level). Next, they asked for courses and referral services run by trained students for their peers. They suggested setting up "rap rooms" in the schools where students could talk about their problems with a panel of trained students and adults, and asked that students who worked in the rap rooms get academic credit for it. The Coalition outlined in detail how the rap room panel should be made up and what procedures they should follow in counseling and making referrals. They made provisions for parental and faculty participation in the program, and drew up guidelines for a training course for all participants. These guidelines covered informational training (human sexuality, the physiology of sex, birth control, abortion and venereal disease) as well as counseling training (interviewing techniques, discussing sensitive subjects, confidentiality,

leading discussions). The Coalition included in its proposal a timetable for implementation of the program, a list of institutions and groups willing to train the program counselors, sources for funding the program, and a list of people and agencies who either helped draw up the proposal or endorsed its goals and guidelines.

This program could never have been brought into the New York public schools if it hadn't been so carefully thought out and presented. As of now, all the schools have put the program into action, and it works well. If you want to know more about the details of the proposals, or want some advice about how to start your own, write to The Coalition for Relevant Sex Education, 300 Park Avenue South, New York, New York.

If you can't get your school board to adopt a proposal like this one, there's always the chance that an individual school might work it into an existing program. Within the New York City public high school system there already existed a peer "rap and referral" program which used high school students who had been trained to provide drug information to other students within particular schools. While the Coalition for Relevant Sex Education was waiting for its proposal to be approved, it decided to get immediate action by working within the "rap and referral" program. A few students within a few schools decided that they should not only sign the Coalition's petition to the School Board, but that they needed the program proposed immediately. At that point they sought out the support of a sympathetic faculty member or two, and took the proposal to the principal, who said either, "Sounds like a good idea—let me take it to the Consultative Council (teachers, parents and students) and see what they say" or "I'm afraid that this isn't the business of education nor the policy of the school—and I'm sure that there would be many parents who would not appreciate the school's becoming involved in this moral issue." (Of course this is a general description, but it does reflect a pattern.)

If the school accepted the proposal, students were trained to make birth control and VD referrals (the Human Resources Administration used some of their staff for training programs). Parents who were reticent or hostile to the program were invited to attend the training sessions. This not only cut down on parental and administrative resistance, but also built a base of support and testimonials from the very people who are often used as excuses by school officials for not having thorough sex education programs.

Chapter Seventeen: Policy

The point of most immediate concern for high school students—on the policy level—is legislation on sex education, contraceptive services to minors, and abortion. A number of students have already been involved in testifying and lobbying, and although it's difficult to determine how successful they've been or what relationship the eighteen-year-

---

"Tomorrow Is Not Inevitable": An Earth Platform

High school students in Connecticut gathered the information which went into this environmental platform; each office-holder and candidate for public office in the state was asked to list his position on each issue in the platform. It was also submitted to Connecticut senators and congressmen, and to Presidential candidates, and was circulated among citizens' groups to use not only as a gauge of candidates and current office-holders, but also a discussion tool. The issues covered by the platform were:

☐. Air Pollution—The platform called on the Connecticut General Assembly to take action to fight air pollution in cities throughout the state.

☐ Water Pollution—The platform called for General Assembly action to regulate clean water standards.

☐ Solid Waste Disposal—The platform recommended a massive state-wide recycling effort.

☐ Urban Environment—The platform recommended proposals that would seek to end urban migration by improving housing and environmental quality in cities, and by promoting long-range planning for expanding communities.

☐ Transportation—The platform urged expansion of mass transit systems throughout the state.

☐ Pesticides—The platform listed the state's needs in the area of pest control, and outlined a system of dealing with them which would be economically and biologically viable.

☐ Energy—The platform proposed a concrete policy for energy conservation that included provision for reduction in the rate of growth for all kinds of energy.

☐ Occupational Health—The platform proposed greater vigilance in the area of occupational health and safety.

☐ Wildlife—The platform demanded legislative action to restore the equilibrium between industrial man and his fellow creatures.

☐ Population Control—The platform suggested using the state's resources to improve the quality of life for the existing population instead of trying to meet the future demands of an unchecked, expanding population.

☐ General Resolutions—The platform endorsed the policy of requiring environmental impact statements from all state agencies undertaking new projects, and it proposed that all public schools in the state incorporate into the curriculum courses covering the topics discussed in the platform.

---

old vote will have on continuing efforts, a group of people in Connecticut have already tried to capitalize on the first teenage-vote election. Connecticut Citizens Action Group brought high school students and trained professionals together to develop and present an "earth platform" on which they asked legislative contenders to stand. Via a whistle-stop tour of high schools, they recruited students to participate in the research and develop-

UNITED NATIONS

ment of a fairly specific statewide environmental platform which would enable voters to obtain commitments from the candidates on specific environmental issues. The platform would provide guidelines for the candidates themselves, and could cut down on the

---

On September 27, 1971, Hariette Surovell had this to say to the Commission on Population Growth and the American Future:

In high school . . . when we get around to discussing venereal disease, a disease which has reached crisis proportions among New York City's young people, we are shown a film about some wholesome 1956 teenage boy who takes a "loose woman" clad in tight pedal-pushers to a motel room. He contracts VD and subsequently infects Sally, the nice girl next door, who wanted to please him because he took her to the expensive country club dance. She breaks out in a rash, sees the doctor, and in a few days her parents are notified. It is a tragic ending with parents and child crying hysterically in the doctor's office. . . .

Because contraception is just not included in the high school curriculum, I made a special request to my hygiene teacher that we discuss it. For one day, the teacher wrote on the blackboard all the methods that she knew. "What method would you recommend to a sixteen-year-old girl?" asked the students. "Sleep with your grandmother," she replied. Incidentally, one of the girls in my hygiene class had a baby approximately ten months later. . . .

I would say that on the average about four girls a week thought they were pregnant, their sisters were pregnant, or their friends were pregnant. Of course, no one was sure. They had absolutely no idea that a simple, low-cost test for pregnancy exists. . . .

How can high school girls be expected to be responsible about using birth control when all knowledge is gotten on the street? . . . It is obvious that the answer to this problem is not to tell the teenagers to stop having sex—it just won't work.

---

mushy pro-environment rhetoric.

Approximately 500 students were recruited. They received a list of experts to contact on a statewide basis, split up into specific task forces, and brought together the results of their studies to produce the platform. At this writing, the platform has been widely distributed in Connecticut—to schools, legislators and citizens' organizations. It's not yet possible to talk about final results in terms of candidates being elected

to the legislature, but it is possible to look at the educational merits of the project in terms of the students who did the research and the people who read the platform.

The Connecticut Citizen Action Group found one way for high school students to influence the way population policy is made. Another way is to testify at any government or agency hearing on the subject; if you have information, or personal insights or recommendations, that you think might influence

(AMERICAN FREEDOM FROM HUNGER FOUNDATION)

MILWAUKEE JOURNAL

policy, come out with it. Hariette Surovell, chairman of the New York High School Women's Coalition, testified before the Commission on Population Growth and the American Future. She told the Commission what the extent of sexual activity, and sexual ignorance, was in her school, and she recommended that relevant birth-control programs

and service referrals be made a part of school practice. In part as a result of her testimony, the Commission came out strongly in favor of confidential services to minors.

In Los Angeles, the group of high school students calling itself YES has been involved in a number of lobbying efforts that should have significant effects on policy. They wrote letters supporting bills relating to VD education and confidential contraceptive services for minors, and both bills passed the California legislature before they were vetoed by the governor. YES students also circulated a peti-

---

When you're thinking about how you can effectively influence policy—whether by petitions or lobbying or testimony—remember that people can have the most influence on the policies and people with whom they're most immediately involved. *The Little Red School-Book* (Soren Hansen and Jesper Jensen with Wallace Roberts, Pocket Books, $1.25), has another good word about influence:

"To have influence it's important to remember

That it's easier to influence someone if you like them and they like you.

That the most influential thing you can do is to be honest (and tactful).

That you need to know the person you want to influence—and to understand why he does what he does.

That a person who's frightened is hard to influence: he often gets angry to hide his fear.

That it's best to bring disagreements out into the open if everybody knows they exist.

That discussing and sorting out disagreements is a good way of learning more about each other. It also helps clear the air.

That if words fail, you can try positive action."

---

tion to protest a Los Angeles Superintendent's Commission recommendation that health classes be removed from the required-courses list in high schools. At the same time YES members were working with local school boards to upgrade the content of health classes. They hand-delivered their signed petitions to the Board of Education, a maneuver which gave the group members a chance to talk about their concerns. An administrative

decision was made not to remove the requirement—a decision which, YES people felt, was a direct response to their activities. Finally, YES convened a statewide gathering of high school students involved with health care concerns to talk with state legislators. At the beginning this meeting consisted mainly of the legislators talking to the high school students, and the group decided that a conference probably wasn't the best forum for doing their

Are You Serious?

If you want to look further into the possibilities for population education, there are several programs for intensive training in the areas of public health, demography, sociology or the behavioral sciences. The following universities offer Graduate Studies and training programs in the population field:

☐ School of Public Health
University of California
Berkeley, California 94720

☐ Carolina Population Center
University of North Carolina
University Square
Chapel Hill, North Carolina 27514

☐ Department of Population Planning
University of Michigan
1225 South University Avenue
Ann Arbor, Michigan 48104

☐ International Institute for the Study of Human Reproduction
Columbia University
78 Haven Avenue
New York, New York 10032

☐ Department of Population Dynamics
School of Hygiene and Public Health
Johns Hopkins University
615 North Wolfe Street
Baltimore, Maryland 21205

☐ International Population and Urban Research
University of California
2234 Piedmont Avenue
Berkeley, California 94720

☐ East-West Population Institute
East-West Center
University of Hawaii
Honolulu, Hawaii 96822

☐ Community and Family Study Center
University of Chicago
1126 East 59th Street
Chicago, Illinois 60637

☐ Population Studies Center
University of Michigan
1225 South University Avenue
Ann Arbor, Michigan 48104

☐ International Population Program
Cornell University
B-5 McGraw Hall
Ithaca, New York 14850

For more information, you may want to look at the *Directory of Population Research and Study Centers in the United States 1972–1973*, a pamphlet published by Planned Parenthood Population, 18 Seventh Avenue, New York, New York 10019. The International Planned Parenthood Federation also publishes a *Directory of Selected Training Facilities in Family Planning and Allied Subjects*. It is available from the IPPF, 18–20 Lower Regent Street, London S.W.1, England.

lobbying. But a day two of the gathering was spent in small strategy groups, made up of students and legislators, where some lively exchanges took place. People talked about what they were doing, shared perspectives, and worked together on where they needed to move. There is still a question at this point as to how much of what was discussed can be translated to a real legislative lobby. But student participants did gain new insights into the possible effects of what they were doing back home.

Part Five: The International Perspective

Chapter Eighteen: What's the Problem?

Action is a child of perception. At the beach, we may see a swimmer waving hello or we may see him signaling for help; we may think whitewashing political shenanigans is illegal or we may consider it merely expedient —and we act somewhat differently according to our perception of a situation.

This chapter is a guide to *a new perspective* in world population issues; it hopes to share with you a perspective of population issues within the context of worldwide development and then, through this perspective, to interest you in effective action. By "action" we mean any of a variety of undertakings—some ambitious, some easy, some education- or policy-oriented—all aimed at alleviating some of the conditions that cause our pressing population problems. We admit that while some of these actions are simple, the framework on which they are based is not so simple. The world is not one-dimensional and neither are the crucial population issues of this world.

The World Tightrope Act

Imagine a line of people holding hands. Imagine further that, although they differ in size and agility, they are walking a tightrope. Many of us see international affairs in this light. We see nations as irrevocably inter-related—forced to hold hands by their dependence on the bonds of world trade, employment and migration patterns, monetary systems, the desire for peace or stability. In turn, each nation, each tightrope walker, has a set of basic needs for energy, food, health, education, etc. Any great imbalance

in one of these bonds or needs and the whole tightrope crew is endangered. One imbalance leads to another. The tightrope walkers might push each other off the wire, unwittingly pull their friends with them or, at worst, all go down together.

The tightrope, like the world, does not shrink or expand; it becomes terribly over-crowded and shaky. The world's poorer nations are, on the average, doubling in size every thirty-five years. This rate of growth (approximately 2 percent per year) severely hinders national development. Other nations, those generally termed "industrialized," are undergoing their own form of explosion—an explosion in consumption. Although the rate of population growth among these countries is relatively low, each child gulps a dispro-portionately large hunk of the world's re sources, leaving little for others. The 18 per-cent of world population in the industrialized nations uses about 80 percent of the world's known resources. Population is one of the key variables in the world-survival balancing act, and the goal is to achieve population size compatible with, and distributed according to, available resources. It is more complicated than it seems, for many nations—and many people within each nation—make decisions which appear to have little or nothing at all to do with population and yet have surpris-ingly strong, often unforeseen, population consequences.

This is our concern: how to deal with the phenomenon of rapid population growth and unequal distribution of world resources. Our

hypothesis is that a substantial part of the solution to world population problems lies in political, economic and social development processes that insure an equal distribution of resources, both among nations and within nations, and that seek to establish conditions of human dignity for all people within the historical and cultural context of each nation. Any effort to provide the benefits of this kind of development to the world's people requires careful planning and management of resources; the current world population will double by the end of the century, and somehow these additional guests at the table will have to be fed, housed, clothed, educated and employed.

If you are not satisfied with the shaky tightrope *status quo*, and want to change some of the conditions that are keeping our planet a demographic mess, you can do something about it, here in the United States. The pages that follow offer three things: a population perspective identifying key issues and targets; models of action which have been successful around the world; and resources— activities, organizations, films, books or whatever—that will help you put your model to work.

Is Family Planning the Answer?

Widespread concern that world population might be increasing too quickly is a fairly recent phenomenon, dating from the 1960's. Early researchers, reasoning that the problem was too many people, primarily focused on finding the most direct and effective means of limiting births—through better contraceptive technology (IUDs, pills, and so on) and through making this technology more easily accessible. While much progress has been made, family planning services around the world are still far from adequate. (In 1973, the International Planned Parenthood Federation researched the extent of unwanted fertility around the world, and found that the most widely-used method of birth control is illegal abortion.)

In addition, the fact that a family planning clinic exists does not mean that every woman in the neighborhood will want to go. What was needed? Better motivation. Many people concerned with population felt that curbing population growth rates depended on motivating parents to want fewer children and on providing them with the education and information to *have* fewer. So the concept of family planning has been expanded to include education, advertising and media coverage, new methods of contraceptive delivery, and incentive programs, as well as sterilization and abortion.

At present there are hundreds of research and information centers around the world working to meet these education and information needs. Government support around the world has increased quickly. Thirty-one developing countries in 1973 maintained official policies favoring family planning to reduce the birth rate and gave support to these programs. Another twenty-eight countries supported family planning but had no such official policy. Even so, the services are still not easily accessible, even in those developing countries supporting family planning, let alone in the fifty or more that do not. Further, family planning programs have seldom reached more than 10 percent of the population they were aimed at. These disheartening facts should not discourage us from doing all we can to expand family planning services—though possibly we expect too much from such programs; there are, in fact, some very persuasive reasons for people (particularly in developing countries) to want to have large families: more help at home, more help in raising other children, security in old age, insurance against the possible death of children.

In this context, family planning should be seen as a method that enables people to achieve the family size they want, no matter how large or small. But what prompts people to want to limit family size? What motivates them? When children enrich life—economically or psychologically—people tend to have many. As the standard of life improves, as women have alternatives to traditional domestic roles, as children become economic liabilities, family size usually tends to decrease. Sometimes, however, when the living standard diminishes, family size decreases, as in the Depression of the 1930's. Conversely, as the standard *improved* after World War II, a "baby boom" took place.

There can be good reasons for having large families—reasons that from our cultural perspective may not make good sense, but that in another kind of society seem to make very good sense. In *Notes From Gorordo Street: A Doctor in Family Planning*, Luz de la Paz Pelaez tells us how it is in the Philippines:

> A couple who had been living with the husband's parents have seven children, all of whom are already in school. We usually have arguments about how much easier it would have been for her if she had limited her children to three or four. "No," she insists. She feels she has taught the children to share responsibility with their parents. For example, the eldest, who will be finishing his training as a pilot, will help the second through school. When the second has finished his course in commerce he will help educate the third . . . This way the whole family will prosper.

> An even simpler reason was voiced by a mother in a family planning clinic in Iran: "When our baby died we were so sad. But I had two more very good little boys. It took away the sorrow of the loss."

In 1963, after extensive study, the United Nations Secretariat formulated a "threshold" thesis, which postulated that when a certain level of economic well-being is reached, family size diminishes. Economic and social progress may indeed have a strong relationship to population limitation. Many of the population control "success" stories have occurred in areas where the majority of the population has started to share the fruits of the nation's progress. In most of these places —Hong Kong, Puerto Rico, Japan, Singapore, Taiwan, and more recently Sri Lanka, Chile, Uruguay, western Malaysia, parts of Egypt, possibly China—birth rates began to drop early in the process of social improvement, often before a large family planning program was fully activated.

Causes and Correlations of Population Limitation

What are some of the factors that tend to weigh in favor of small family size and low fertility? Researchers have begun to identify some of these socio-economic variables, although the precise mix and the levels at which they become significant appear to vary.

Healthy children and low infant death rate seem to be preconditions for smaller family size. Here is a paradox little appreciated by those who "blame" modern medicine for the population explosion. Parents who are not certain that their children, especially males, will survive—whether because of the effects of childhood illness or malnutrition—tend to have more children to compensate for possible deaths. While childhood death rates have decreased in practically all the world's countries, the decrease is uneven —poorer families have sickly children and higher death rates.

Education by itself does not make smaller families, but increasing levels of education are correlated with lower fertility. Innovations take hold in a literate population. Higher education levels for women are of particular

importance.

Another important influence on family size is the availability of decent jobs—which means not only work to do, but a just return for that work. The classic image of a family in a developing country pictures the farmer father, the older daughters taking care of the younger ones, the sons trying to earn a little money at the local market, everyone helping in the fields—just to eke out a bare subsistence. With this employment pattern, children help to maintain the family and provide income, often at astonishingly early ages. When a family rises above this subsistence level to a point at which adequate land, some income and some education are assured, then family size tends to be lower.

At certain levels—in the government policy-making arena, for example—religion can affect family planning programs and population issues. But at the individual and family level, religion does not seem to exert as much influence on fertility as other factors. Italy and France, both Catholic countries, have much lower population growth rates than Indonesia, which is Muslim, Thailand, which is Buddhist, or Venezuela, which is Catholic.

Development and Population

Better health care and nutrition, employment opportunities and rising income, improved education, literacy, and higher economic and social status for women are factors that, in themselves, do not change population. Rather, together they bring a more equitable distribution of a society's resources, opening up opportunities for the individual, more freedom, more control over personal destiny, opportunities to indulge in new attitudes and innovations. Family planning is one of those innovations.

The estimated one and a half billion people who go to sleep each night hungry or malnourished are living on the brink. In a real sense, poverty also costs them their freedom. They cannot afford innovation—life is too desperate. Only when people can plan their lives as a whole can they be expected to plan their families in an effective manner. Says a family planning doctor, "Poor people, when enlightened about family planning, will readily accept methods which are simple, easy and inexpensive, like the IUD and the pills. Religion is not a deterrent. The difficulty lies in sustaining their interest in family planning after they have accepted it. Poverty, inadequate food and inadequate health care demand solutions more urgent than family planning. Economic and social development should go hand-in-hand with family planning; the prospects of a bright future through family planning alone are dim."

Development that can successfully relieve population pressures requires the distribution of its economic and social benefits to a majority of people rather than to a small elite. Education, for example, can be used to benefit either the elite or a large proportion of the citizenry. Investment in labor-saving machinery may help the urban elite, but may increase unemployment among the poor. Food, income, employment opportunities,

Selected Bibliography on Population and Development

This is a list of the best available literature on the subject—all of it easily obtainable by mail from the source, or from your bookstore.

PAMPHLETS AND PERIODICALS

A New Development Strategy? Greater Equity, Faster Growth, and Smaller Families. Robert F. Hunter, James P. Grant and William Rich. Overseas Development Council, 1717 Massachusetts Ave., N.W., Washington, D.C. 20036.

Smaller Families Through Social and Economic Progress. William Rich. Overseas Development Council, Suite 501, 1717 Massachusetts Ave. N.W., Washington, D.C. 20036.

Rural Development, Income Distribution, and Fertility Decline. James E. Kocher. Occasional Paper of the Population Council 1973, distributed by Key Book Service, Inc., 425 Asylum St., Bridgeport, Conn. 06610.

Population. Valerie Kincade Oppenheimer. Headline Series No. 206, Foreign Policy Association, 345 East 46th St., New York, N.Y. 10017.

Rethinking Economic Development. Robert Shaw. Headline Series No. 208, Foreign Policy Association, 345 East 46th St., New York, N.Y. 10017.

Youth and Population: Report of the Working Party on Youth and Population. United Nations Center for Economic and Social Information, United Nations, New York, N.Y. 10017.

Development Forum. Monthly periodical of the United Nations Center for Economic and Social Information, United Nations, Palais des Nations, Geneva, Switzerland.

The New Industrialist. Monthly magazine available from R.P.S. Ltd., Victoria Hall, London, S.E. 10, England.

BOOKS

Development Reconsidered. Edgar Owens and Robert Shaw. Lexington Books, D.C. Heath and Company, Lexington, Mass. 1972.

The Cruel Choice. Denis Goulet. Atheneum, New York, N.Y. 1971.

World Development: An Introductory Reader. Helene Castell, ed. Macmillan, New York, N.Y. 1971.

The Challenge of World Poverty. Gunnar Myrdal. Random House, New York, N.Y. 1970.

Partners in Development: The Report of the Pearson Commission. Praeger, New York, N.Y. 1969.

In the Human Interest: A Strategy to Stabilize World Population. Lester R. Brown. W. W. Norton and Co., Inc., New York, N.Y. 1974.

health care services—all can be distributed in relatively equitable or inequitable ways.

Population Growth Versus National Development

When people are healthier, happier, not in need of child labor, not terribly fearful for old age security, they can afford to limit family size. Rapid population growth, however, hinders social and economic development.

Some say that population growth is the primary cause of poverty and underdevelopment. Boiled down to the basics, the controversial issue is this: which must come first, slower population growth or general economic and social development? This is worse than the chicken-and-egg argument—and almost as old.

The answer is that both must come first. Population problems may be symptoms of

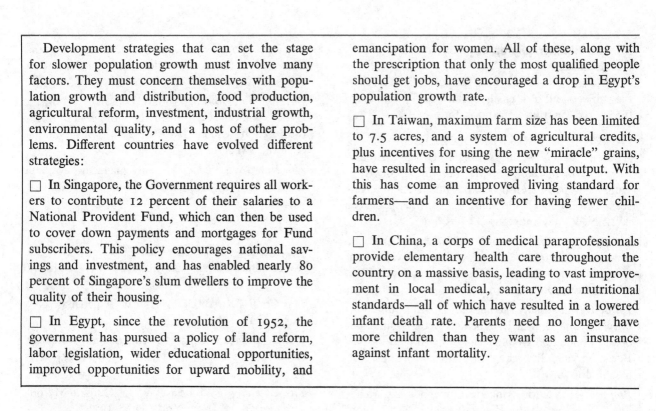

Development strategies that can set the stage for slower population growth must involve many factors. They must concern themselves with population growth and distribution, food production, agricultural reform, investment, industrial growth, environmental quality, and a host of other problems. Different countries have evolved different strategies:

☐ In Singapore, the Government requires all workers to contribute 12 percent of their salaries to a National Provident Fund, which can then be used to cover down payments and mortgages for Fund subscribers. This policy encourages national savings and investment, and has enabled nearly 80 percent of Singapore's slum dwellers to improve the quality of their housing.

☐ In Egypt, since the revolution of 1952, the government has pursued a policy of land reform, labor legislation, wider educational opportunities, improved opportunities for upward mobility, and emancipation for women. All of these, along with the prescription that only the most qualified people should get jobs, have encouraged a drop in Egypt's population growth rate.

☐ In Taiwan, maximum farm size has been limited to 7.5 acres, and a system of agricultural credits, plus incentives for using the new "miracle" grains, have resulted in increased agricultural output. With this has come an improved living standard for farmers—and an incentive for having fewer children.

☐ In China, a corps of medical paraprofessionals provide elementary health care throughout the country on a massive basis, leading to vast improvement in local medical, sanitary and nutritional standards—all of which have resulted in a lowered infant death rate. Parents need no longer have more children than they want as an insurance against infant mortality.

certain developmental problems, but they are symptoms which make the patient sicker. It is a circular process, and employment opportunities, maternal and child health, improved status for women, land redistribution, are all population polices.

Creating the Conditions for Development and Population Stabilization

Unfortunately, the realities of social and economic change can't be reduced to a formula, and in trying to create the developmental conditions that will slow population growth, there is no simple generalization, no single approach that fits all countries.

In general, successful development strategies involve basic structural changes in the society, but development strategies vary from country to country, from culture to culture. No single political structure can provide the sole answer for national development or population: development approaches vary greatly. Yet development must come from within —no foreign help will suffice when there is no national will to make fundamental changes. We cannot "do" development for someone else, any more than we can solve the population problems of other countries.

Too often, in the past, the very word "development" has meant chiefly the introduction of the western pattern of energy-intensive mechanized industry, which may merely swell

unemployment, promote urbanization, increase pollution, exhaust resources and destroy the people's way of life. There is, fortunately, a growing realization in some quarters that the Western development pattern is not necessarily the best for underdeveloped nations.

It may come as a surprise to learn that we in the United States and in industrialized nations are hindering many development efforts, or are nurturing—perhaps unwittingly —many of those structures that are antithetical to world development. World eco-nomic and social improvement requires basic structural changes in the developing and developed nations, and we in the U.S. must do our share.

Granted, we have many problems in this country, but we cannot therefore ignore the development needs of the rest of the world. We are living in a global village, where two-thirds of the village is a ghetto and where 20 percent of the villagers control 80 percent of the village's wealth. We have a moral imperative to do something about this situation—and a pragmatic imperative as well.

International Trade and International Development

If you're interested in reading more about world development as it relates to trade issues, you might try the following pamphlets from the Overseas Development Council (1717 Massachusetts Ave., N.W., Washington, D.C. 20036):

The Developing Countries in a Changing International Economic Order: A Survey of Research Needs. James W. Howe, ed. 1973. (81 pages) $1.00

Adjustment Assistance, American Jobs, and Trade With the Developing Countries. Charles R. Frank. 1973. (49 pages) $1.00

Special Drawing Rights and Development: $10 Billion for Whom? James W. Howe. 1972. (16 pages) 50¢

Other good resources are:

UNCTAD III: Make or Break for Development. A Special World Development Movement Report on the United Nations Conference on Trade and Development. World Development Movement, 69 Victoria Street, London SW1H, England.

End of an Illusion: Verdict on UNCTAD III. Report of the World Development Movement. World Development Movement, 69 Victoria Street, London SW1H, England.

Help or Hindrance: Aid, Trade, and the Rich Nations' Responsibility to the Third World. David Millwood. SODEPAX (Committee on Society, Development and Peace of the World Council of Churches), 15 Route de Ferney, 1211, Geneva, Switzerland.

The stable, affluent markets of the world are relatively few in number. We could trade a good deal more with developing countries if they were more economically advanced and able to afford our manufactured goods and absorb some of our raw materials into their industries. We are endangered by their poverty, for poverty breeds conflict—and conflict is something we still have no world mechanism to resolve. All these issues beg enlightened U.S. involvement with international economic and social development. We *can* help set some of the conditions that will make world problems more solvable.

International Trade

International trade agreements and tariffs, which are generally initiated by industrialized nations, make it virtually impossible for poor countries to do their own manufacturing for export or to process much of their own raw material. The burden of a tariff need not fall more heavily on the poor than the rich, but that is usually what happens. President Nixon's "temporary" 10 percent surcharge on processed imports (goods from other countries) was meant to keep German and Japanese goods out of the American market where they were competing—all too successfully—with American goods; but in the process it has hurt the fledgling industries of the poorest countries—industries which by and large have seldom been a threat to U.S. businesses. What could we do instead to encourage industry in the poorer countries while protecting American factories and jobs? We could provide satisfactory adjustment assistance to workers and communities being threatened by foreign imports, and at the same time lower tariff walls.

This course of action, if carefully planned, would strengthen the U.S. economy in the long run and allow some poor countries to develop their fledgling industries, which are so vital a part of overall economic and social development.

Poor countries also lose out when it comes to international trade agreements. More than four-fifths of the total foreign exchange for poor countries comes from their exports; thus trade provides the main thrust for improving the standard of living. Yet, poorer countries, never adequately represented at multilateral trade negotiations, tend to lose out in attempts to change the current world order. Current patterns of trade perpetrate the preservation of neo-colonial empire and economic privileges—keeping the poor nations producing primary products. Here what is needed is a policy change at the highest levels; the needs—and possible contributions—of the developing countries should be considered carefully in all international trade negotiations.

Multinational Corporations

Multinational corporations are the newest and among the more confusing of dominant global institutions. The biggies among the multinational corporations are more powerful than some countries. Gross annual sales of General Motors, Standard Oil and Ford, for example, are each greater than the gross national product of Norway, Austria and Hungary.

It has become fashionable in some circles to view those large corporations as cosmic pigs, but this simple-minded generalization is not true and it avoids one very important issue: How can multinational corporations be harnessed to deal effectively with human problems and social needs? How can their potential for stimulating trade, creating jobs and fostering new industries in the poor countries be realized?

There are some hopeful beginning points: one interesting way of spreading the benefits of commerce is by industrial complementation agreements whereby one thing may be produced in many countries. Very simply, the corporation can make economic use of different countries while creating jobs as well as products. Good points go to Ford for its proposed complementation agreements to make a small car in Asia by setting up production centers for different components in Singapore, Thailand, Taiwan, Indonesia, South Korea, Malaysia and India.

Bad points go to those corporations that take out of the poor country's economy more than they invest. In general, U.S. corporations with interests in Latin America have repatriated as much as twice the amount that has been invested by the U.S. private sector or from U.S. foreign aid funds. Clearly those countries cannot afford that loss.

Bad points also go to those corporations that interfere with the governments or dabble in the internal politics of the poor nations—often with the aid of a rich nation's government. The close working relationship of government and business poses some particularly

"When we come before the heavenly Father and He says, "Did you feed them, did you give them to drink, did you clothe them, did you shelter them?" and we say, 'Sorry Lord, but we did give them .3 percent of our gross national product,' I don't think it will be enough."

Barbara Ward

difficult problems. On the one hand, the government of the rich country feels, not without some justification, that it must protect the interests of its citizens overseas. On the other hand, the developing country is often powerless to regulate the local branch of a multinational corporation—particularly when the corporation is backed by the enormous clout of a big foreign government. Against this combination—big business and big government—the developing country is powerless.

The point is that some multinational corporations have grown enormously without corresponding accountability. They are fully answerable neither to any individual country nor to their owners, who often number in the tens of thousands of stockholders. They should have stronger, more responsive, publicly acknowledged guidelines set by the country of origin or an international body.

What role do the multinational corporations play with respect to population? First, by affecting the economy of a region, they affect population distribution, and probably overall growth rates. Second, in the choices they make between capital-intensive investment (big machines, few jobs) or labor-intensive investment (few machines, many jobs), they affect local economy, family economy and population growth. The choice be-

tween imposing one bulldozer and hiring 100 unskilled laborers has profound implications for the quality of life in developing countries. If this choice interests you to the point where you want to do some further reading on the subject, we refer you to an excellent United Nations report, *Multinational Corporations in World Development*. It's available from the United Nations, New York, N.Y. 10017, and the sales number of the report is E73IIA2.

Foreign Policy and Foreign Aid

A third area where richer nations can help set the stage for sound international development and confrontation of population problems is the field of foreign assistance. Generally, foreign assistance takes the form of loans and grants—for commodities, technical help and program support within developing countries. The primary sources of these loans and grants are: government foreign assistance programs, private foundations, international organizations such as the United Nations, and international financial institutions such as the World Bank.

One of the most abused labels in the public conscience must be "foreign aid"; yet foreign aid is a very necessary instrument in promoting world development. First, a few facts: in the name of foreign assistance, the U.S. gov-

If the work multilateral organizations are doing in the population field interests you, you might want to look into the subject further. Some good books and pamphlets on the subject exist, among them:

The United Nations and the Population Question. Richard Symonds and Michael Carder. McGraw-Hill, 1973. 236 pp.

Population, the Multilateral Approach. United Nations Fund for Population Activities. New York: UNFPA, 1972.

Questions and Answers. United Nations Fund for Population Activities. New York: UNFPA, 1973.

Report, 1969-1972. United Nations Fund for Population Activities. New York: UNFPA, 1972.

Recently the International Planned Parenthood Federation began to publish *People*, a quarterly journal of articles, book reviews, and discussions on developments in the population field. It is available in English, French and Spanish from IPPF, 18-20 Lower Regent Street, London W 1, England. IPPF also publishes a newsletter, *IPPF News*.

Three more sources of information were developed for World Population Year 1974, a major undertaking of the United Nations system. They include:

World Population Year Bulletin. United Nations Fund for Population Activities. 485 Lexington Avenue, New York, N.Y. 10017.

A Matter of People. Dom Moraes. New York, Praeger, 1974.

Dialogue on Population. A film by Roberto Rosselini. Available from UNFPA, 485 Lexington Avenue, New York, N.Y. 10017.

---

ernment provides not only military aid, but loans (which must be paid back) and grants (which are not repayable) to governments and organizations in developing countries, to U.S. institutions sponsoring projects in developing countries, and to international organizations for their work. That work covers a wide range: health, education, agriculture, nutrition, and so on. Contrary to myth, the U.S. assistance program is not a huge giveaway. In comparison to the aid programs of other governments, the U.S. ranks twelfth—after Australia, Belgium, Canada, Denmark, France, Germany, the Netherlands, Norway, Portugal, Sweden and Great Britain—in the proportion of government budget spent to promote economic and social development. Nor is foreign aid a real sacrifice to U.S. taxpayers, for we profit nicely from it. The Agency for International Development (A.I.D.) reports that in fiscal year 1972, A.I.D. development programs had a net favorable effect on the U.S. balance of payments. In that year 80 percent of A.I.D. spending for development assistance went to buy U.S. goods and services, and the development assistance program actually resulted in a net flow to the U.S. of $32 million. Add to this the fact that half our "aid" is really in the form of loans which must be repaid with some interest, and it becomes evident how a poor country can actually lose money on aid.

Nonetheless, our aid programs—when intelligently conceived and administered—can work for the good of developing countries. In South America, the growth of cooperatives is due in large measure to U.S. efforts, as is the system of agricultural credits now prevalent in some Southeast Asian countries.

But what role can U.S. government assistance play in shaping the population policies of the poor countries? The small army of population program afficionados has been debating this question for years. Lately the participants in the debate have included development experts and foreign governments. Currently the U.S. government spends about $125 million annually for population programs around the world—almost entirely in the form of grants. These include substantial contributions to the United Nations Fund for Population Activities, to U.S.-based foundations and nonprofit organizations such as the Pathfinder Fund, The Population Council, and university centers in the U.S. The population program financed by U.S. aid is almost entirely a family planning effort: fostering family planning services, birth control education and information, delivery of contraceptives and biomedical research into birth control and reproduction. Critics of the program often claim that it is too narrowly conceived and puts too much money into a small field. Defenders of the program say that more money is needed in order for the results of good family planning measures to be seen around the world.

How can the U.S. government aid program be made more responsive to the development and population needs of other countries? One way would be to separate military from development assistance. There is no reason why development assistance aimed at narrowing the gap between the rich and poor should be included in the same legislation with military and defense aid. But, in fact, more than a third of the Foreign Assistance Act legislation requests are for military aid to Vietnam, security assistance and the infamous Contingency Fund (which pays for training police, among other things). A relatively simple separation of such incompatible elements of legislation would make U.S. motives less suspect overseas, and would make it easier to assess our financial commitment to economic and social development in other countries.

Another way to improve our assistance programs would be to end the requirement that U.S. assistance monies be "tied" to U.S. purchases. Recipient nations should be able to purchase their own goods—from the cheapest supplier. Multilateral loans and aid (from organizations like the U.N.) are not tied to purchases from any one country, and the increasing U.S. support of these multilateral channels is generally to be applauded. To improve the quality of U.S. assistance, loans and grants should be made on at least a two-year basis. Development assistance should no longer be a dumping ground for our political aspirations and excess commodities.

It is also vital that more attention be paid to job development in labor-rich countries. The U.S. has high labor costs, and use of technology can often result in industrial savings. The poor countries have plentiful supplies of labor, but little expensive technology and capital. Consequently A.I.D. and devel-

---

Population and Foreign Aid

Further readings on the issue of U.S. foreign assistance and world development include these government publications for your prospecting:

U.S. Aid to Population/Family Planning in Asia. Report of a Staff Survey to the Committee on Foreign Affairs, U.S. House of Representatives, Ninety-Third Congress, 1st Session, February 25, 1973. U.S. Govt. Printing Office, Washington, D.C. 20402.

U.S. Foreign Assistance in the 1970s: A New Approach. Report to the President from the Task Force on International Development, March 5, 1970. U.S. Govt. Printing Office, Washington, D.C. 20402. (30¢)

Population Program Assistance: Aid to Developing Countries by the United States, Other Nations, and International and Private Agencies. AID Bureau for Population and Humanitarian Assistance, Office of Population, Washington, D.C. 20523. December 1972. U.S. Govt. Printing Office, Washington, D.C. 20402. ($3.35)

Program Presentation to the Congress. Agency for International Development: FY1974. AID, Washington, D.C. 20523.

In addition, you might take a look at the following:

International Assistance for Population Problems: Recipient and Donor Views. Report of the Organization for Economic Co-Operation and Development, Paris, France, 1970.

Population: International Assistance and Research. Report of the Organization for Economic Co-Operation and Development, Paris, France, 1969.

World Population Crisis: The United States Response. Piotrow, Phyllis Tilson. New York: Praeger Publishers, 1973.

---

opment agencies should emphasize use of labor, not capital; creation of jobs, not employment of big U.S.-built machines. A.I.D. has too often concentrated on capital-intensive, not labor-intensive, development.

Finally, the government must develop a sane, comprehensive domestic population policy for the U.S. if it is to encourage other governments to develop such policies. Many of the criticisms leveled against our national family planning programs—that they are aimed only at the poor and the blacks, that they are discriminatory or even genocidal in intent—are being reiterated at the international level.

"Population" means much more than family planning and abortion. Unless people achieve a certain level of well-being, all the condoms and pills in the world will fail to halt rapid population growth and unbalanced, uncharted population distribution. If family size limitation can be shown to be conditional on some social reform, economic development or agricultural advance, then that should become an integral part of the population program. For example, family size limitation in some countries is affected by better education; therefore, aid to education should be integrated with population programs. In some areas, slowing population growth is predicated on improved health of mothers and children, so maternal and child health should be developed vigorously with the population effort. Family planning doesn't stand alone,

it's part of a much more complicated development fabric.

Multilateral Organizations

The United Nations, the World Bank and related organizations are new, growing forces on the world scene, and all have parts to play in planning and distribution for development and population programs. These organizations are, increasingly, recipients of foreign assistance funds from the rich nations. Once received, funding is used *multilaterally*—as needed for Third World development by the international organizations which are, ideally, responsible to no single government. This transition, from the bilateral nation-to-nation foreign assistance of ten years ago to the increasing use of international organizations in coordinating world development efforts, has been widely praised.

The United Nations Fund for Population Activities is the main channel for multilateral funding of the population programs. The Fund was established in 1967 in response to an increasing awareness within the United Nations system that a number of developing countries needed technical assistance for population activities and wanted it to be channeled to them through the U.N. The Fund began its major operations toward the end of 1969, and in four years has disbursed $120 million for 800 projects in more than ninety countries. (In the next few years this spending will increase to a rate of $75-$100 million a year.) Despite this activity on the part of UNFPA, three-fourths of international assistance for population activities still goes through bilateral channels. As the role of UNFPA increases, the volume of assistance being provided through bilateral programs may diminish. This is a healthy development, both from the point of view of the recipient governments, which want assistance through multilateral channels, and from the point of view of the donor governments, because routing of assistance through multilateral channels eliminates the suspicion that the donors are involved in population activities for their own ends. This kind of multilateral population assistance encourages the recipient governments to develop their own policies and programs, which can range from demographic studies (like that being undertaken in Egypt), family planning programs (like the one being instituted in Thailand), a census (like the one Nigeria is taking), maternal and child health care programs (like that being put to work in Chile), to studies of migration patterns (like the one Indonesia has undertaken) or vasectomy programs (like the one India is developing).

The United Nations Fund for World Population Activities is not the only multilateral population organization. The International Planned Parenthood Federation, which was established in 1951, is a coalition of national family planning associations. It has grown in the size and in the scope of its programs as interest in family planning activities has grown around the world. In 1951 it had twenty-one national affiliates. Today it has more than eighty. Its budget has gone up from less than $100,000 in 1953 to more than $25 million in 1973. Most IPPF programs concern research, training and family planning delivery systems; but the international federation is becoming increasingly involved in information, education and communication programs.

Unfortunately, the work of multilateral organizations like UNFPA and IPPF is dependent on the good faith of the donors. In some cases promised donations have not been forthcoming, and for that reason, two very innovative financial institutions may be floundering. One of these, the International Development Association, is an affiliate of the World Bank. It gives loans to poorer countries, generally payable in fifty years at three-fourths of one percent service charge, with a ten-year grace period in payments. This provides an important source of capital for the poorest of the world's nations, but it may soon dry up for lack of money. The U.S. promised to contribute 40 percent of the necessary funds—a woefully small amount—but in 1973 the U.S. Congress refused to honor even this commitment.

If multilateral aid for development programs is to succeed—and it deserves to succeed—then all the contributing nations must fulfill their financial commitments to the organizations involved.

It should be clear by now that we in the United States have many opportunities to influence—for good or ill—the development programs, and therefore population trends in other countries. That we must do so is a certainty, for we are all aboard what economist Barbara Ward calls Spaceship Earth, and our ability to survive depends on our being able to adjust the inequalities in the distribution of population and resources. Yet in large part the American public has chosen to turn its back on this increasingly desperate international situation. It has done little or nothing—and that nothing is a vote for perpetuating current conditions. This is where we come in.

There are things we can do to affect issues —to change current conditions. The targets include the general public, corporate shareholders, government officials, church leaders, directors of foundations—and many others.

How to get at them, and how to effect some changes, are the subjects of the following pages.

Chapter Nineteen: Bringing It Home

The first problem you have to face in trying to do anything about international population programs is that nobody at home cares very much about them, or knows very much about them. Many Americans, confronted with a picture of a malnourished child in Bangladesh, will respond by saying, "Well, it's all tragic, of course, but if they'd just stop having all those children there wouldn't be a problem." It's a long way from that kind of attitude to successful population action, and the first step on the road is some effective kind of public education, or consciousness raising.

Using the Occasion

Often consciousness raising takes place when someone says something unexpected and provocative in the middle of what might have been a totally predictable meeting, conference, seminar, class or conversation. Suddenly new issues, real issues, are raised and discussed. This happened at the African Population Conference, held in December, 1971 in Accra, Ghana, when several young participants met and presented a controversial paper entitled, "A New Approach to Population Research in Africa: Ideologies, Facts, and Policies," an independent paper which generated considerable debate. The conference was sponsored by the U.N. Economic Commission for Africa (ECA) and the International Union for the Scientific Study of Population (IUSSP) with support from the International Planned Parenthood Federation (IPPF). It attracted the luminaries of African demography and family planning, and well-known representatives of international and national foundations and agencies were all there. The young participants argued that many demographic "facts" are actually the products of unexamined biases and ideologies of population research; that population growth is repeatedly and wrongly overemphasized as an independent variable separable from other elements of the development process; that to view all social ills as curable by population control is unrealistic; that African self-development was being throttled, not fostered, by prevailing patterns of production which cause African rural areas to stagnate, urban areas to fill to overflowing with cheap, unskilled labor, and a country to be drained of its resources for the benefit of rich foreign nations; and that it is indeed a narrow view of population policy that limits it to fertility control and emphasizes family planning for purposes of national interest rather than individual benefit. The paper generated enormous controversy at the conference, and started all the participants thinking about the issues that were raised.

The same sort of thing happened at one of the most learned population conventions in the United States—the annual meeting of the Population Association of America. Three young graduate students presented a radical critique of what was, in the authors' opinions, the racist, imperialist mentality of U.S. population organizations and international population assistance, and their views generated a great deal of provocative discussion. (The North American Congress of Latin America has since reprinted the article for distribution. It is available as "Population Control in the Third World," by William Barclay, Joseph Enright and Reid T. Reynolds, reprinted in the *NACLA NEWSLETTER*, Vol. LV, Number 8, December 1970; it can be ordered from NACLA, Box 57, Cathedral Park Station, New York, New York 10025.)

In both these instances, the key to effective consciousness raising was the timing and the quality of the target audiences. With proper timing and a reasoned presentation, different points of view can receive great attention and have considerable effect on the policies under deliberation. If you are a student, question your professor during a class discussion. Write to and approach local politicians. Next time you have a term paper to complete, do a little research on development issues and present your findings to the class.

Posters and Handbills

"I am not a racist, but . . . . " "I have nothing against colored people." "They certainly do have rhythm!" All these are phrases from a consciousness-raising program involving posters that took place at a university in Great Britain. During the first week of classes at the opening of the school term, posters were plastered all over the university—with slogans which were reminiscent of phrases used by those who refuse to admit their own racial prejudices. Many of the posters carried political cartoons, which were both funny and politically striking. This is the sort of educational program that works—the audience

was clearly defined (faculty and students), the medium could not be ignored (posters), and the message was as direct as possible.

Another consciousness-raising action in Great Britain involved the distribution of handbills at a factory where coffee beans were processed. One evening as workers were leaving for home, students handed out single-page leaflets describing the conditions in the countries where coffee beans came from (in this case Kenya, Ethiopia and Colombia) and the basic issues behind international trade (e.g. the rise in prices for the instant coffee produced in the factory as compared to the fall in prices which the developing countries could charge for their exports). It was not an emotional document and made no mention of exploitation or colonialism. It simply described what was happening, and ended by saying that it was nice to be the lucky ones who have gained but it was only fair that a more stable and just price be negotiated with the producer countries, especially in the light of their development problems, even if this negotiation meant that the rich would have to accept a lower profit. This was a single action which the student did not intend to follow up, but several days after the action the students received a letter from the factory asking for more copies of the handbill. Subsequently, the students and the Trade Union organizers, as well as the factory workers, met for discussion on global development issues. Over a long term, such discussions can prove highly satisfactory in political consequences.

Street Theater

Street theater is a way of communication, a way to tell people what you are concerned about, whether it's world poverty, unemployment, trade, or whatever. You can get your message across in a way that's interesting for both you and your audience—people are more likely to watch a play or short scene than to read a leaflet.

Street theater involves acting out a simple plot. The "actors" aren't on stage, or anywhere far from the audience, because they want people to join in by asking questions, making comments. Street theater is an engaging drama. There is no "us" (actors) and "them" (audience). Performances take place on the street, in parks, shopping centers, school auditoriums, rock concerts, festivals —anywhere that people pass by and aren't in too much of a hurry; anywhere that people are waiting. Street theater can happen at meetings, after church, during the lunch hour at school. (Get permission from the authorities when necessary.)

To start street theater, first get a small group of interested people together to discuss and decide on the subject of the drama. Then gather all the information you can about the subject and talk it over. Decide on your "message." This may take some time, but it's essential to know exactly what you want to say. Then decide how to dramatize the idea. Look at the political cartoons in the papers for ideas you can adapt to fit your subject. Write a rough outline of what's going to happen. Either write a script or improvise by acting it out together. Practice. Make it funny or dramatic. You may want to exaggerate and add new props, costumes and funny lines as you go along. Show it to friends and get their comments. Decide on a location where you will be seen and heard properly. When you are confident, do it. Remember that you want to get bystanders involved in discussion; one way to do this is to give them leaflets supplementing what you're acting out. Don't be afraid of experimenting; later, if you give a repeat "performance," you can cut out the parts that didn't work, or add to the scenario where you feel it needs amplifying.

Remember to keep the plot simple. If you think you won't be heard, mime the plot, and have a narrator with a mike. Be careful that you don't get in each other's way while acting —but you don't have to follow complicated rules about movements as if you were on stage. Try to have a pattern for the action so people see what's happening; make sure there's plenty of movement from one part of your "stage" to another, but always take care that this movement means something. You could, for instance, place one actor up high somewhere (perhaps on a ladder) to show he's "on top," or you could have everyone move toward one side of the "stage" where there's something interesting to see. Make props and labels BIG. Exaggerate costumes. Wear ordinary clothes so you don't look like actors—use bits of costumes: a hat, a cloak, part of a uniform. Have labels on people as well as on things. Symbols—especially simple ones—are important in street theater. For props you could collect a loaf of bread, a stepladder, toy guns, charity collecting tins, posters, hand puppets, etc. Make a giant boot out of papier-mâché (to show people being trodden on), or money bags made out of fabric, stuffed, with big dollar signs on the outside. Anything goes, so long as its meaning is clear.

Here is one simple idea for a play: a man (rich-looking) is suffering from guilt because of world poverty. He sits moaning with pain. A doctor comes along and diagnoses "guilt." A large label marked GUILT is placed on him. The doctor says, "What you need is an inoculation of my special GIVE A FEW PENNIES TO THE POOR mixture." He gives him an injection from a giant syringe. The man recovers and goes off happily. But the next patient (a large globe labeled WORLD) is still sick, and another doctor says that they still can't afford the medicine to cure him. End with the line "Who are we trying to cure?" Leaflets follow, asking that question, and pointing out that action for development has to concern itself with modifying underlying structures that cause poverty and be based on an intellectual conviction of the necessity for this kind of change.

In summation, street theater is essentially an allegorical genre of drama. Symbols and suggestive dramatizations are key tools in this kind of theater. One caveat is in order, however; street theater can degenerate to simple didactic moralism with too little drama and too much dogma. The *object* of street theater should be to provoke thought and discussion, and not to preclude them.

Film Series

A film series is an excellent way to raise consciousness. It can be organized around a specific topic (several examples follow), or a group may choose to show one or two films dealing with poverty in the U.S. and an equal number about global poverty. This second alternative may be better for a group just getting started. It is easier to organize because films that are locally available can be used, which may save time and money. In addition, it is faithful to a basic principle of development education: domestic and global development are interrelated and part of one process.

Careful selection of films is important. Many films which are available are inaccurate, outdated and reinforce stereotypes and ethnocentric attitudes. (A poor film can, however, be an opportunity for a good learning experience, if its weaknesses are discussed.) A publication of the American Freedom from Hunger Foundation which may help you to select films is *A Guide to Films About Development*. All the films listed in this section are described in the guide. Also helpful is the International Planned Parenthood Federation's catalog of population films and audio-visual aids.

Be sure to order films one or two months before the film series begins. Schedule the film series for a regular time and place before ordering the films, so that you can select alternate viewing dates. You may decide to charge admission to cover the cost of renting films. Often good films can be obtained free from the public library. Have a teacher check the films available through the public school system audio-visual department, or have a student at the local university obtain films from the university film library. Distribute flyers giving the dates and film titles to high school, college, church and other groups. The purpose of the film-discussion series should be clearly articulated in all publicity. Preview the film, preferably with the speaker, if you have invited one.

Your film series can also include discussions after each film is screened; such discussions might deal with the way the films relate to each other, what they say individually and collectively. You could also increase the educational impact of your film series by distributing or suggesting readings after one film discussion so that participants will come better prepared for the next. It is also possible to structure an entire course around a film series, with readings, lectures and discussions supplementing the screening of films on a given subject.

Multi-Media Shows

You can create multi-media "happenings" —which are a great stimulus to consciousness raising—by using common materials (such as advertisements) in an unusual way. A half-dozen people sitting on a living room floor, listening to the radio and record player and looking through old magazines for slide material, could construct the basis for a slide and tape presentation. Clip pictures, advertisements and phrases from magazines and newspapers and some songs. Coordinate the slides and music and you have a show to turn on people in a church congregation, a school assembly, a workshop, teach-in, etc. Slide shows are an effective and economical medium which reach your public in a direct way.

One way to put together a slide show would be to scan magazines, cutting out every advertisement or phrase using the word "world" in it. Do the same with words like "nation" or "love." Cut out pictures of families playing together, of riots, of student protests, of poverty. Make slides (using chalk on black paper) giving facts and figures, comparing expenditures for war with expenditures for international development; gross national product with foreign aid funding; population predictions to the year 2000, and similar figures. Find magazines showing astronauts or space photographs of earth. Then put together a tape of music and dialogue discussing the "Spaceship Earth" perspective from the moon.

If your community has had a Walk for Development (see page 172), compile th slides from the Walk, the projects you funded, and slides made from newspaper clippings and of other development themes to create a development presentation. If you have a film, throw it on the center screen of a three-projector presentation, showing wing slides of development needs around the world. Or project the film on the ceiling. Instead of using the soundtrack of your film, just put on a tape or rec-

---

If the idea of simulation games excites you, you may want to consider a few more model games already proven successful by other groups. One source for these is "A Bibliography of Education Simulations Available for Rent from the Church Center for the United Nations," a listing of eighteen games related to international affairs. It's available free from the Church Center for the United Nations, 777 United Nations Plaza, Room 10E, New York, New York 10017. Or try William A. Nesbitt's *Simulation Games for the Social Studies Classroom*, published by Thomas Y. Crowell, Inc., 201 Park Avenue South, New York, New York 10003. This is probably the best single book on the subject; it has a twelve-page appendix listing most available games and telling where to purchase them. However, the author does not mention the cost of the games. The book costs $2.50.

---

ord of your choice.

If you are not familiar with photography, find someone who is. For details of the technical equipment and processes needed for sound and light recording, you'll need the advice of someone who knows, but the basic ingredient in preparing any presentation is a vivid imagination.

A good multi-media presentation is a product of experimentation and innovation. Its flexibility and simplicity make it a mind-grabbing tool for community groups. The key is starting off slowly, thinking out what you want to say and why you want to say it. Don't be afraid to use shock tactics, but make sure that you're painting an accurate development picture. (Be able to substantiate your statements and statistics.) Your first show may be just ten minutes long, using only a hundred slides and one projector. By the end of a year, you may have 2000 slides and three thirty-minute presentations on three projectors. Tinker around and see what works in your community. Remember, there is an *infinite* variety of multi-media presentations you and your group can create.

Simulation Games

A simulation game is a consciousness-raising tactic which actively involves the people participating. The players are more than passive observers—they can experiment and test ideas, and try on other points of view. In deciding whether to plan a simulation game, a role-playing incident or guerrilla theater—all are similar in some ways—you must decide on your purpose. Simulation games are solely concerned with the players themselves, while guerrilla theater is primarily concerned with conveying a message to an audience. Role playing may do both. Simulation games for twenty to forty players can be used effectively in workshops, classes in school, seminars, teach-ins and discussion groups. They help people learn more about development issues and to get to know each other—they even affect attitudes, enabling players to try out skills and learn new concepts.

Most simulation games require several hours of playing time. The subsequent discussion, the "debriefing," is an essential part of the game. In debriefing sessions, participants analyze the game critically and discuss

Street theater, film series, multi-media presentations, simulation games and other actions are all described in greater detail in some of the following publications:

Development: Bridge to Peace. Kathleen Desmond. American Freedom From Hunger Foundation, 1717 H St., Washington, D.C. 20006.

Target: Development Action. American Freedom From Hunger Foundation, 1717 H St., Washington, D.C. 20006.

Community Encounter: Programme Models for the Community. Canadian Council for International Co-Operation, 75 Sparks St., Ottawa, Ontario, Canada.

Action/Communications: The Creation of Multi-media—Multi-Screen Presentations by Community Groups. Canadian Council for International Co-Operation, 75 Sparks St., Ottawa, Ontario, Canada.

The Development Puzzle: A Sourcebook for Teachers. Nancy Lui Tyson, ed. Voluntary Committee on Overseas Aid and Development, 69 Victoria St.,

London SW 1, England.

Intercom #69: Development: New Approaches: A Guide for Educators with Issues and Resources. Center for War/Peace Studies, 218 East 18th St., New York, N.Y.

Ideas and Action Bulletins. Freedom From Hunger Campaign—Action for Development, Food and Agricultural Organization, Rome, 00100, Italy.

Development Education Exchange. Freedom From Hunger Campaign—Action for Development, Food and Agriculture Organization, Rome 00100, Italy.

Action Pack for World Population Year. PAC Ltd., Stage House, High Street, Benson, Oxfordshire, England.

Population Action Pac. World Assembly of Youth, 39-41 Rue d'Arlon, Brussels, Belgium.

Guide to Student Action for Development. World University Service (WUS) and the International Student Movement for the United Nations (ISMUN), 5 Chemin des Iris, Geneva, Switzerland.

how it illustrates (or does not illustrate) the real-life situation, how they felt during the game, what their roles were, and so on.

One such game that has been played successfully by many groups is *Baldicer*, a game in which a "food coordinator" is responsible for the survival of 150 million people. The game deals with the questions of world food production, distribution and trade. Though one may dispute how well the numerical equivalents of various factors illustrate the real-life situation, this game always initiates discussion of underdevelopment and its causes. (To order it, send $25 to John Knox Press, Box 1176, Richmond, Virginia 23209.)

The Money Game is a provocative simulation of the economic interactions between developed and developing nations. In this game, a special conference has been called by Ghana to deal with the crisis in trade for developing countries, and during the course of play ethical imperatives for use of power and wealth in relation to development may become explicit. (The game was published in March 1970 *Concern* magazine, which may be ordered from *Concern*, 475 Riverside Drive, Room 401, New York, New York 10027, at 25¢ per copy.)

All these games are mere suggestions, and

you may get your best results with simulations
you make up yourself. Try anything to see if
it works—if you succeed in provoking discussion, raising new issues or changing minds,
you're well on your way.

Chapter Twenty: Doing Something About It

It isn't easy for an individual or a group to make any impact on United States foreign policy, or on the priorities and perceptions of international assistance organizations. But there are some things you can do to make a dent in the population problem abroad, just as there are things you can do about it at home. Changing attitudes, raising consciousness—all this is one step. You can carry your convictions further by taking positive action. You, and anyone else you or your group can persuade to follow your example, can make yourselves heard.

Self-Tax

One model for action is the self-tax. You can make an individual decision to reduce your income by a fixed amount or percentage each year, and the amount saved is a self-tax which goes to help development or population projects. How much you tax yourself is up to you. You could decide to pledge $3 each month to a specific development project, which would be a self-tax per year of $36. Or you could decide to pledge, say, 2 percent of your income and channel it through a development agency. You then figure out your annual income and pay out 2 percent. Suppose you have an income in 1974 of $6,000. Rapid calculation on your internal IBM computer shows that 2 percent of 6,000 comes to $120 per year. This is the same as $10 a month—so your self-tax is $10 a month. Let's say you get a raise at the end of 1974 so that your income in 1975 is going to be $9,000. You go back to the computer and figure out that 2 percent of $9,000 is $180 per year, which is $15 per month. So for 1975 your self-tax is $15 a month.

Where the money goes depends entirely on what the organizers of the self-tax scheme decide. Most of the self-tax schemes now operating in Europe provide their funds to development projects, both international and domestic. The self-tax is most effective when the person joining the scheme has a choice of where his or her money should go. A group could set up a self-tax scheme with a choice of four development or population-related projects. The funds would then be divided among the projects in accordance with the individual choices made by those participating in the self-tax scheme. The self-tax money could also be used for educational purposes.

The key to the success of self-tax schemes is getting many people involved. It may be heroic if you are self-taxing yourself at 99 percent of your income, but if you are alone it's not much use. Form a self-tax union, a group of more than 100 people, drawing in contributors from the ranks of high school and college students, parents, teachers, businessmen, professionals, church congregations —everybody. The initial aim of a self-tax campaign is to form more than 100 unions, *i.e.*, involve more than 10,000 people. A hundred unions can produce an annual income of over $250,000 per year. But this is not all—another exciting part of the self-tax idea is the chance it offers for meeting with people and discussing development on a one-to-one level. The idea cannot spread by mail-

The 3W1 Experience

Successful self-tax schemes are already underway in Britain, Germany, Sweden, Denmark, Holland, Switzerland and Australia. The exact formula varies —but most are percentage schemes. In Switzerland, the members of the Berne Declaration Group pledge 2 percent of their incomes. In Britain, members of Third World First (3W1) pledge any amount between 1 percent and 3 percent. Total world membership of development self-tax schemes, not counting church schemes, is probably around 80,000 people.

The experience of the Third World First group in Britain is probably the most relevant. 3W1 started in 1969 with two Oxford College students. The self-tax idea spread quickly in Oxford, involving some 1,000 students within three weeks. By July of 1970, some 15,000 British college students had joined 3W1, and today's membership is over 25,000—which is 8 percent of Britain's total college population. The students are contributing an average of $10 per year to international development and educational projects. 3W1 has organized an educational arm, which puts out the Third World File, a folder of basic development documents, and *The New Internationalist*, Britain's only popular development magazine (available from R.P.S. Ltd., Victoria Hall, London SE 10, England). 3W1 has active college groups all over Britain and supplies them with films, speakers and campaign ideas. 3W1 organizers visited Algeria last summer to gain some direct experience of conditions in one important Third World country. Besides expanding its base among college students, 3W1 is now making deliberate efforts to reach out into the wider community. For more information, contact Third World First, 4 Marston Ferry Road, P.O. Box 59, Oxford, England.

ings or casual discussions. People do not commit themselves to the self-tax principle without seriously looking at the ideas behind it. To involve someone in the self-tax scheme you have to talk with them, discuss, argue the case for development. This means you have to be well-informed. During the discussion you have to combat all the hoary old arguments with the facts. This means you are doing an educational job. Many people don't know what "development" is and have little feeling for international and domestic problems. But they have to take seriously someone who comes to see them and asks to spend some time discussing the issues. The self-tax scheme puts development in the context of a specific campaign, and it tests your ability to communicate what you know successfully.

Spreading the self-tax is not easy, but it will expose you to all the rationalizations that people use to shrug off their responsibility. You have to respond to these rationalizations creatively, and thus "shoot them out of the sky."

Every person joining the self-tax scheme must receive a series of good educational materials. One of the best features of the self-tax scheme is the fact that someone who has joined by committing his money on a regular basis has a built-in incentive to study the materials he receives. Those who are organizing the recruitment of new people to join the self-tax scheme also have a prime incentive to educate themselves on the issues. Without this education they will not be able to persuade anyone that development is worth fighting for!

The main justification for a self-tax scheme is as a means of getting people involved in development issues. While the self-tax scheme can raise large amounts of money, there are certainly more effective fund-raising techniques. The strengths of the self-tax scheme are these: the people getting involved are taking on a small but definite long-term commitment; it is a strong educational tool; it is a way of involving people who would otherwise stay out of the issues or else simply toss a few pennies in a bowl for the starving; and it offers a specific organizational focus in which people can work and succeed in proportion to their efforts.

In building up a self-tax union to the level of 100 people or more, the first technique you need is mastery of the "friend to friend" system. Say there are six people involved at the start. They want to build up to 100. First they adopt the self-tax for themselves—signing the self-tax forms. Then each one involves five friends. This builds the membership to thirty-six. A meeting is then held of all thirty-six members (or as many of them as possible). At this meeting, all the ideas of the self-tax scheme are thoroughly discussed and the new members get excited about expanding membership.

This is where the second technique comes into play—the setting of a target. For example, the group could set a target of 70 in three days' time and 150 in ten days' time, with two meetings scheduled to take place in three days and ten days. Everybody present at the meeting must take responsibility for involving at least two more people by the next meeting. It's then up to the organizers to really work hard to involve new members, to keep phoning existing members to get them into action, and to meet the targets. The great advantage of this is that everyone has something to aim for. As targets are achieved, people become more and more confident that they can go on to achieve more. The campaign is exciting because many people are involved.

Other Models for Action

Sometimes the most effective action you can take is the kind that gets someone else to do something. One such action is the Walks for Development sponsored by the American Freedom From Hunger Foundation. Each year there are hundreds of these walks, in which people walk twenty-five miles and seek donors who pledge so much per mile. Total revenue from a walk is collected and sent to development projects, domestic and overseas. The AFFHF publishes an international catalogue with over 150 development projects to guide local Walks for Development committees in their project selections, and it also operates an extensive educational program here in the U.S. (For more information on Walks for Development write: AFFHF, 1100 17th Street N.W., Washington, D.C. 20036.)

A more radical way to influence the situation is to boycott companies which support conditions in a country that can directly hinder development. A boycott of such a company can be a means of forcing a corporation to change its policies, to become more consistent with development objectives. But be careful when you're considering such an action, and weigh the issues carefully. Often the issues are complex—corporate investment and other policies can also *assist* development.

A boycott is merely a vehicle to change the nature of American involvement—to refrain from intervention and oppression. The crux of a boycott's success lies in its educational aspects.

Boycott tactics vary greatly. Leafletting and talking to shoppers at the entrances of stores form one way to communicate to people about a corporate policy or investment, but don't forget the importance of publicity in newspapers, radio and television talk shows. And other effective tactics are mock trials (guerrilla theater) on corporation policy, as well as teach-ins.

All these activities may seem to have little to do with overpopulation in India, or urban overcrowding in southeast Asia; and yet they are the prerequisite for any sort of sane thinking about population throughout the world. It would be useless, as well as offensive, for you to embark on a campaign for the distribution of birth control pills in an area where no one has enough to eat, or to donate funds to establish a family planning clinic in a village where leprosy, beriberi or cholera are a greater threat to the people than a rising birth rate.

Our world tightrope act will come to a sorry end unless each of us does something to ensure that each man and each woman have the freedom to determine the essential conditions under which he or she must live. That is what world development is all about—or what it should be about. And that is what these action models, and consciousness-raising exercises, are aimed toward.

A Final Word

Throughout this book we have tried to give you the tools for creative action on population issues, and to that end we have outlined some programs, suggested references, and listed resources that will be of help to you in your own thinking and planning. These models and resources do not by any means exhaust the possibilities for innovative action; they are meant to get you started. We hope that you'll use your own imagination in adapting the suggestions in this book to your own needs and situations. Remember that action is not so much a matter of circulating petitions, showing movies or distributing literature as it is a matter of getting results—through these efforts and others. A better understanding and appreciation of population issues among all communities and groups, a more active involvement of concerned individuals in population programs, a closer link between what goes on here and what's happening in the rest of the world—these are results worth working for.

Bibliography

Throughout this handbook we have listed countless books, pamphlets, magazine articles and newsletters that have specific things to say in areas of special interest. The following short bibliography is therefore a rigorously selective one; it consists of a few titles that can be thought of as a cornerstone for your population research. They are the essential works in the field.

The American Population Debate, Daniel Callahan, ed. Doubleday, 1971. 375 pp.

Is There an Optimum Level of Population? Papers presented at the American Association for the Advancement of Science Symposium, December, 1969. Singer, S. Fred, ed. McGraw-Hill Book Co., New York, 1971.

Population: A Clash of Prophets. Edward Pohlman, ed. New American Library, New York, 1973. 492 pp.

Population/Resources/Environment: Issues in Human Ecology. Second Edition. Paul R. Ehrlich and Anne H. Ehrlich. W. H. Freeman, San Francisco, California, 1972. 383 pp.

Population: Quantity vs. Quality. Shirley Foster Hartley. Prentice-Hall, Inc., Englewood Cliffs, New Jersey, 1972. 341 pp.

Principles of Demography. Donald Bogue. John Wiley and Sons, New York, 1969. 917 pp.

Psychological Perspective on Population. James T. Fawcett, ed. Basic Books, Inc., New York, 1973. 522 pp.

Social and Economic Correlates of Family Fertility: An Updated Survey of the Evidence. Norman H. Lowenthall, Research Triangle Institute, Research Triangle Park, North Carolina, 1973. 109 pp.

Index